Masai

Travel Guide

Unveiling the Wonders of Wildlife, Culture, and Adventure

Fernando A. Carlos

TABLE OF CONTENTS

~ 4 ~

Masai Mara visitation story

During my recent trip to Kenya, I had the incredible opportunity to visit the renowned Masai Mara National Reserve. Known for its breathtaking landscapes, abundant wildlife, and vibrant Maasai culture, this visit was a dream come true for me. As our safari jeep entered the reserve, I was immediately captivated by the vastness of the grassy plains that stretched as far as the eye could see. The golden hues of the savannah created a picturesque backdrop against which the wildlife seemed to come alive. The air was filled with anticipation, and I couldn't wait to spot some of Africa's most iconic animals. Within minutes of our arrival, we encountered a majestic herd of elephants leisurely grazing in the distance. Their enormous size and graceful movements left me in awe. As we continued our journey, we spotted giraffes gracefully munching on the treetops, their long necks bending effortlessly.

The real highlight of our visit was witnessing the Great Migration—an awe-inspiring natural phenomenon that sees over a million wildebeests, zebras, and gazelles travel across the Mara in search of greener pastures. The sight of this massive herd on the move was a sight to behold. Dust filled the air as hooves thundered across the plains, creating a spectacle that was both thrilling and humbling. Our skilled guide took us to prime locations, strategically positioning the jeep to offer us the best views of the wildlife. We saw prides of lions lazily basking in the sun, their manes glowing against the backdrop of the vast landscape. Cheetahs stealthily patrolled the grasslands, their slender bodies built for speed. And, of course, the elusive leopard made a brief appearance, camouflaged amidst the trees, displaying the true beauty of the Masai Mara's biodiversity. The Masai Mara not only offers incredible wildlife encounters but also provides a unique opportunity to engage with the local Maasai people. We visited a traditional Maasai village and were warmly welcomed by the community. The villagers shared stories about their rich cultural heritage, demonstrated their vibrant traditional dances, and showcased their intricate beadwork and handicrafts.

It was a privilege to learn about their way of life and witness their deep connection to the land and its wildlife. Each day in the Masai Mara brought new adventures and surprises. From breathtaking sunrises that painted the sky with vivid hues to the spine-tingling sounds of hyenas and lions echoing through the night, it was an experience that awakened all my senses. The nights were spent around a campfire, listening to the stories of fellow travelers and exchanging tales of our encounters in this magical place.

As I reluctantly bid farewell to the Masai Mara, I couldn't help but feel a profound sense of gratitude for the privilege of witnessing nature's grandeur up close. The memories of this visit will forever be etched in my heart, reminding me of the beauty and resilience of the animal kingdom and the importance of preserving these natural wonders for generations to come.

History of Masai Mara

The history of Masai Mara is intertwined with the rich tapestry of the Maasai people, who have inhabited the region for centuries. The Maasai are a semi-nomadic ethnic group known for their strong cultural traditions and deep connection to the land. Long before the establishment of the Masai Mara National Reserve, the Maasai roamed freely across the vast savannah, living in harmony with the abundant wildlife that thrived in the region. Their traditional way of life revolved around cattle herding, and they developed a deep understanding of the land, its resources, and the animal species that coexisted with them.

In the late 19th century, European explorers and colonizers arrived in East Africa, including the area that is now known as Kenya. The Maasai faced significant challenges during this period, as their lands were encroached upon and their traditional lifestyle was disrupted. However, the Maasai fiercely defended their territory and maintained their cultural identity despite external pressures. In 1948, the Serengeti National Park was established in what is now Tanzania, encompassing a vast area that extended into Kenya. The land in Kenya was later designated as the Masai Mara Game Reserve in 1961. The reserve was named in honor of the Maasai people and the Mara River that flows through it.

Over time, the Masai Mara Game Reserve evolved into a globally renowned wildlife conservation area, drawing visitors from all over the world to witness the incredible biodiversity and witness the annual Great Migration. In 1974, the reserve was expanded and officially became the Masai Mara National Reserve, covering approximately 1,510 square kilometers (583 square miles) of pristine wilderness.

Today, the Masai Mara National Reserve stands as a testament to the conservation efforts and the resilience of the Maasai people. It is a protected area that showcases the incredible diversity of African wildlife, including lions, elephants, leopards, cheetahs, giraffes, and countless other species. The reserve also serves as an important economic hub for the surrounding communities, providing opportunities for tourism, employment, and sustainable development. Efforts are made to involve the local Maasai communities in the management and conservation of the reserve, recognizing their deep knowledge and cultural connection to the land.

The history of Masai Mara is a story of coexistence, preservation, and appreciation for the natural world. It is a testament to the enduring legacy of the Maasai people and their unwavering commitment to safeguarding the land and its magnificent wildlife for generations to come.

Welcome to Masai Mara

Welcome to Masai Mara, a land of breathtaking beauty and abundant wildlife! As you step into this extraordinary destination, you are about to embark on an adventure that will leave an indelible mark on your soul. Prepare to be captivated by the vastness of the Mara's iconic savannah, stretching as far as the eye can see. The golden grasses sway gently in the breeze, inviting you to explore the wonders that lie within. The air is infused with a sense of anticipation, as if the very essence of the wilderness is calling out to you. As you venture deeper into the reserve, you'll discover a world teeming with wildlife. Majestic elephants roam freely, their colossal presence commanding respect. Giraffes elegantly graze on acacia leaves, their long necks defying gravity. Zebras, with their striking black-and-white stripes, paint a mesmerizing picture against the backdrop of the plains. But it is the Great Migration that truly defines the Masai Mara. Witness the awe-inspiring sight of a million wildebeests, zebras, and gazelles as they traverse the

Mara River in a courageous quest for greener pastures. The thundering hooves, the swirling dust, and the raw determination of these animals will leave you in awe of nature's grand spectacle.

The Masai Mara is not just a sanctuary for wildlife; it is also a vibrant tapestry of culture and traditions. The Maasai people, known for their rich heritage, welcome you with open arms. Immerse yourself in their way of life, learn about their ancient customs, and experience the beauty of their traditional dances and songs. Engage in conversations with the Maasai elders, and gain a deeper understanding of their harmonious coexistence with the land and its creatures.

Whether you're an avid wildlife enthusiast, a nature lover, or simply someone seeking a profound connection with the Earth, the Masai Mara offers an experience that is beyond compare. From the captivating sunrise that bathes the landscape in warm hues to the symphony of wildlife sounds that echo through the night, every moment spent here will be etched into your memory. As you embark on this unforgettable journey, remember to tread lightly and respect the delicate balance of nature. Take the time to marvel at the intricate ecosystems, to appreciate the interconnectedness of all living beings, and to forge a deep connection with this untamed paradise. Welcome to Masai Mara, where the wild reigns supreme and the beauty of the African wilderness will leave an everlasting imprint on your heart.

Geography and Climate of Masai Mara

The Masai Mara is a region of mesmerizing geography and a climate that sets the stage for a thriving ecosystem. Located in southwestern Kenya, it forms part of the larger Mara-Serengeti ecosystem, which stretches across the border into Tanzania. Let's delve into the fascinating geography and climate of the Masai Mara.

Geographically, the Masai Mara is characterized by vast, rolling grasslands that extend as far as the eye can see. These golden plains, interspersed with scattered acacia trees and rocky outcrops known as kopjes, create an iconic and picturesque landscape. The Mara River winds its way through the reserve, providing a lifeline for the abundant wildlife that calls this region home. The reserve sits at an average elevation of around 1,500 meters (4,900 feet) above sea level, contributing to its moderate climate. The altitude brings cooler temperatures compared to other parts of Kenya, offering a pleasant escape from the sweltering heat.

The Masai Mara experiences two distinct seasons: the dry season and the wet season. The dry season, which generally occurs from July to October, is known as the peak tourist season. During this time, the weather is characterized by warm days, cool nights, and minimal rainfall. The lack of vegetation and the scarcity of water sources force wildlife to gather around permanent water sources, creating excellent game viewing opportunities. The wet season in the Masai Mara typically extends from November to June. It is divided into two phases: the shorter rains (November to December) and the long rains (March to June). These periods bring much-needed precipitation, transforming the plains into a lush green oasis. The landscape bursts into life as the grasses grow taller and the wildflowers bloom, attracting a wealth of herbivores and birdlife. The wet season offers a different but equally captivating safari experience, with opportunities to witness the birth of young animals and observe migratory bird species.

It's important to note that the weather in the Masai Mara can be unpredictable, and variations can occur even within a single day. Mornings are typically cool and crisp, while afternoons can be warm, often reaching temperatures of around 25-30 degrees Celsius (77-86 degrees Fahrenheit). Nights tend to be cooler, with temperatures dropping to around 10-15 degrees Celsius (50-59 degrees Fahrenheit). It's advisable to pack layers of clothing to accommodate the varying temperatures throughout the day. The Masai Mara's unique geography and climate have fostered a diverse ecosystem that supports an incredible array of wildlife. From the iconic big cats to massive herds of wildebeests, zebras, and gazelles during the Great Migration, the Masai Mara offers an unrivaled opportunity to witness the wonders of the natural world.

So, whether you visit during the dry season when the animals congregate around water sources or during the wet season when the plains burst with vibrant life, the geography and climate of the Masai Mara combine to create an unforgettable safari experience that will leave you in awe of nature's splendor.

Reasons to visit Masai Mara

There are numerous compelling reasons why visiting the Masai Mara should be at the top of your travel bucket list. From its iconic wildlife to its rich cultural heritage, here are some of the most enticing reasons to visit the Masai Mara:

Extraordinary Wildlife

The Masai Mara is renowned for its exceptional wildlife encounters. It is home to a diverse array of species, including the iconic African Big Five (lions, elephants, leopards, rhinoceros, and Cape buffalo). Witnessing these majestic creatures in their natural habitat is a truly awe-inspiring experience. Here are some more details about the exceptional wildlife you can expect to see in this incredible destination:

i.   **Big Cats:** The Masai Mara is famous for its population of big cats, including lions, leopards, and cheetahs. Lions roam the savannah in prides, showcasing their majestic presence and powerful hunting skills. Leopards, known for their elusive nature, may be spotted lounging in trees or stealthily navigating the grasslands. Cheetahs, the fastest land animals, showcase their incredible speed as they chase down prey.

ii. **Elephants:** The Masai Mara is home to a significant population of elephants. These gentle giants can be seen peacefully grazing on the grasslands or taking refreshing baths in the Mara River. Observing these magnificent creatures up close is an awe-inspiring experience that highlights their intelligence and social bonds.

iii. **Wildebeests, Zebras, and Gazelles:** The Great Migration is a key attraction of the Masai Mara, with millions of wildebeests, zebras, and gazelles embarking on their annual journey. Witness the thundering herds as they navigate the perilous Mara River, braving crocodile-infested waters and facing predators along the way. This spectacle of survival and endurance is a testament to the resilience of nature.

iv.   **Rhinoceros:** The Masai Mara is also home to both black and white rhinoceros, two endangered species that are under constant threat from poaching. Spotting these magnificent creatures in their natural habitat is a privilege, as they play a crucial role in maintaining the delicate balance of the ecosystem.

v.   **Giraffes:** The Masai Mara boasts a healthy population of giraffes, known for their graceful movements and towering presence. Witness these gentle giants as they elegantly feed on acacia leaves, their long necks bending effortlessly to reach the treetops.

vi.   **Hippos and Crocodiles:** The Mara River is teeming with hippos and crocodiles. Observe these fascinating creatures as they bask in the sun or submerge themselves in the river's cool waters. The river crossings during the Great Migration offer a thrilling opportunity to witness the interactions between the migrating animals and these formidable predators.

vii. **Abundant Birdlife:** The Masai Mara is a haven for birdwatchers, with over 450 bird species recorded in the area. From the regal African fish eagle to vibrant species like lilac-breasted rollers and superb starlings, the Mara offers an incredible variety of avian life. Whether you're a seasoned birder or a novice enthusiast, the region provides ample opportunities to observe and appreciate these feathered wonders.

The Masai Mara's extraordinary wildlife offers a glimpse into the beauty and diversity of the natural world. From witnessing epic predator-prey interactions to marveling at the gentle giants that roam the plains, every wildlife encounter in the Masai Mara is a testament to the intricate web of life that thrives in this remarkable ecosystem. Prepare to be captivated by the untamed beauty of the animal kingdom and create memories that will last a lifetime.

The Great Migration

One of the world's greatest natural spectacles, the Great Migration, occurs in the Masai Mara. Witness millions of wildebeests, zebras, and gazelles embark on a treacherous journey across the Mara River in search of greener pastures. The sheer scale and drama of this event are unmatched, making it a must-see phenomenon for nature enthusiasts. Here's more about the Great Migration and why it's a must-see event:

i. **Scale and Numbers:** The Great Migration involves the movement of millions of wildebeests, zebras, and gazelles across the vast plains of the Masai Mara and the Serengeti. Witnessing the sheer numbers of animals involved is mind-boggling, as these massive herds stretch as far as the eye can see, creating an unforgettable visual spectacle.

ii. **Perilous River Crossings:** One of the most thrilling aspects of the Great Migration is the river crossings, particularly at the Mara River. The migrating herds must navigate through treacherous waters, where lurking crocodiles lie in wait. Witnessing the desperate attempts of the wildebeests and zebras to cross the river without being taken by the powerful jaws of the crocodiles is a heart-pounding and dramatic experience.

iii. **Constant Movement and Drama:** The Great Migration is a perpetual cycle of movement, with the herds constantly seeking fresh grazing lands and water sources. As they journey through the savannah, they face numerous challenges, including predators such as lions, cheetahs, and hyenas. The dynamics and interactions between the migrating herds and the resident wildlife create a captivating drama that unfolds before your eyes.

iv. **Survival of the Fittest:** The Great Migration is a prime example of the survival of the fittest. Weak or injured animals fall prey to predators or succumb to exhaustion during the arduous journey. Witnessing the raw power of nature as predators seize opportunities and the herds band together to protect themselves is a humbling experience that highlights the delicate balance of life in the wild.

v. **Birthing and the Circle of Life:** The Masai Mara is witness to the remarkable phenomenon of birthing during the Great Migration. As the herds arrive in the fertile lands of the Mara, pregnant females give birth to their young, ensuring the next generation continues the cycle. Witnessing newborn calves and foals taking their first steps is a tender and poignant experience that underscores the resilience and hope of the animal kingdom.

vi.   **Year-round Migration:** The Great Migration is not a singular event but a year-round phenomenon. The precise timing and route of the migration vary depending on the availability of water and grazing. This means that no matter when you visit the Masai Mara, you have a chance to witness different stages of this remarkable journey, offering a unique experience with each visit.

The Great Migration in the Masai Mara is a testament to the awe-inspiring power of nature and the inherent instincts of wild animals. It is a testament to their resilience, adaptability, and the innate drive to survive. Being a witness to this natural spectacle is a humbling and unforgettable experience, immersing you in the extraordinary cycles of life and the wonders of the animal kingdom

Unparalleled Safari Experiences

The Masai Mara offers exceptional safari experiences. Traverse the vast savannah in a 4x4 vehicle or enjoy a hot air balloon ride for a unique aerial perspective. Professional guides and trackers enhance your experience, providing in-depth knowledge and ensuring remarkable wildlife sightings. Here's more about the safari experiences that make the Masai Mara truly exceptional:

i. **Game Drives:** Game drives are the quintessential safari experience, and the Masai Mara offers some of the best game drives in Africa. Climb aboard a 4x4 vehicle, accompanied by expert guides and trackers who possess an intimate knowledge of the reserve. Explore the vast savannah, traversing different landscapes and encountering a wealth of wildlife. From thrilling predator-prey interactions to close-up encounters with the iconic Big Five, game drives provide a front-row seat to the drama and beauty of the animal kingdom.

ii. **Hot Air Balloon Safaris:** Experience the Masai Mara from a different perspective by taking to the skies in a hot air balloon. Drift gently above the plains, enjoying panoramic views of the sweeping landscape and the animals below. The stillness of the early morning hours, accompanied by the breathtaking vistas and the sense of freedom, creates a truly magical experience. Conclude your balloon safari with a champagne breakfast in the bush, creating memories that will last a lifetime.

iii. **Walking Safaris:** For a more immersive and intimate experience, embark on a walking safari. Accompanied by knowledgeable guides, set off on foot to explore the smaller details of the bush. Learn about animal tracks, identify bird species, and discover the intricacies of the plant life. Walking safaris offer a deeper connection with nature, allowing you to appreciate the subtleties of the ecosystem and experience the thrill of being on the ground where the wild animals roam.

iv. **Night Game Drives:** The Masai Mara also offers the opportunity for night game drives, where you can explore the reserve after sunset. Equipped with spotlights, venture into the darkness to witness nocturnal animals in action. Encounter elusive creatures such as leopards and hyenas, and witness the vibrant nightlife of the African savannah. Night game drives provide a different perspective and reveal a whole new world that comes alive under the cover of darkness.

v. **Conservation and Research Initiatives:** The Masai Mara is at the forefront of conservation efforts and research initiatives. Some safari lodges and camps offer opportunities to participate in these projects, providing a deeper understanding of conservation challenges and the measures being taken to protect the ecosystem. Engage with conservationists, learn about anti-poaching efforts, and contribute to the preservation of this remarkable landscape.

vi.   **Sundowners in the Bush:** As the sun begins to set over the Masai Mara, indulge in the tradition of sundowners. Sip on refreshing drinks while soaking in the breathtaking vistas of the savannah. The colors of the sky transform into a palette of golden hues, creating a serene and magical atmosphere. Sundowners offer a moment of tranquility and reflection, allowing you to appreciate the beauty of the wilderness as day turns into night.

Safari experiences in the Masai Mara offer a unique blend of adventure, education, and immersion in nature. Whether you choose to embark on game drives, take to the skies in a hot air balloon, or explore on foot, each experience provides a different perspective and an opportunity to connect with the wild. Prepare to be captivated by the sights, sounds, and wonders of the African bush as you embark on unparalleled safari experiences in the Masai Mara.

Cultural Immersion

Engage with the Maasai people, one of Africa's most iconic ethnic groups. Explore their villages, learn about their traditional way of life, and gain insights into their deep connection with the land and its wildlife. Witness their vibrant dances, experience their warm hospitality, and appreciate their intricate beadwork and handicrafts. Here's more about the cultural immersion experiences that make the Masai Mara truly special:

i. **Maasai Villages:** Visit a Maasai village and interact with the local community. Gain insights into their daily routines, traditions, and customs. Learn about their unique pastoral lifestyle, characterized by cattle herding and a deep connection to the land. Engage in conversations with the Maasai people, listen to their stories, and witness their vibrant dances and traditional ceremonies.

ii.   **Traditional Dwellings:** Experience the traditional Maasai dwellings known as "manyattas." These structures, made of sticks, mud, and cow dung, offer a glimpse into the Maasai's architectural heritage and their sustainable way of building. Learn about the materials used, the construction techniques, and the significance of these dwellings in Maasai culture.

iii.   **Cultural Demonstrations:** Immerse yourself in Maasai culture through captivating demonstrations. Watch as Maasai warriors showcase their remarkable jumping skills, an integral part of their traditional dances and ceremonies. Witness beadwork demonstrations and learn about the symbolism and cultural significance of the intricate designs.

iv.   **Traditional Cuisine:** Indulge in the flavors of authentic Maasai cuisine. Sample traditional dishes such as nyama choma (grilled meat), ugali (a staple made from maize flour), and sukuma wiki (collard greens). Participate in cooking demonstrations to learn about the preparation methods and the cultural importance of food in Maasai society.

v.   **Handicrafts and Markets:** Explore the vibrant Maasai markets and browse the array of handicrafts. Admire the exquisite beadwork, leatherwork, and intricate jewelry crafted by Maasai artisans. Engage with the artisans, learn about their techniques, and perhaps even purchase a unique piece as a memento of your cultural immersion experience.

vi. **Community Projects:** Some lodges and camps in the Masai Mara are involved in community development projects that support education, healthcare, and sustainable livelihoods for the Maasai people. Participate in these initiatives and contribute to the local community. Engage in educational programs, visit schools, or support women's empowerment projects, gaining a deeper appreciation for the challenges and aspirations of the Maasai community.

vii. **Cultural Exchanges:** Engage in cultural exchanges with the Maasai people, sharing your own traditions and learning from theirs. Take part in language lessons, traditional music and dance sessions, or even spend a night in a Maasai homestead, participating in the rhythms of their daily life.

Cultural immersion in the Masai Mara allows you to go beyond the wildlife and delve into the soul of the Maasai people. By connecting with their traditions, understanding their challenges, and appreciating their unique way of life, you gain a profound appreciation for their rich cultural heritage. Embrace the opportunity to engage with the Maasai community, for it is through these interactions that you truly understand the significance of cultural diversity and the importance of preserving indigenous cultures.

Photographic Opportunities

With its stunning landscapes and diverse wildlife, the Masai Mara is a photographer's paradise. Capture breathtaking sunrises, dramatic wildlife encounters, and the raw beauty of the African wilderness. Whether you're a professional photographer or an amateur enthusiast, the Masai Mara offers endless opportunities to capture truly remarkable images. Here's more about the photographic experiences and highlights that make the Masai Mara a dream destination for shutterbugs:

i.   **Iconic Wildlife:** The Masai Mara is renowned for its diverse and abundant wildlife, providing endless opportunities to capture stunning images. From the majestic lions and cheetahs to the graceful giraffes and powerful elephants, the variety of animal species in the Mara ensures that every shot is unique. Capture the raw beauty, expressions, and behaviors of these incredible creatures in their natural habitat.

ii. **Great Migration:** The Great Migration is a photographer's dream, offering dramatic and captivating scenes. Witness the massive herds of wildebeests, zebras, and gazelles as they traverse the plains, creating a visual spectacle. Photograph the river crossings, where thousands of animals navigate through crocodile-infested waters. Capture the intensity, chaos, and emotions of this remarkable migration, freezing moments in time that tell a story of survival and instinct.

iii. **Landscapes:** The Masai Mara's landscapes are breathtakingly beautiful, providing a stunning backdrop for your photographs. The vast savannah, dotted with acacia trees and dramatic escarpments, offers endless possibilities for capturing wide-angle shots that showcase the immensity of the region. The golden hues of the grasslands at sunrise and sunset create a magical atmosphere, while the expansive skies and cloud formations add depth and drama to your compositions.

iv. **Golden Light:** The Mara's positioning near the equator ensures that the lighting conditions are often ideal for photography. The golden hour, occurring during sunrise and sunset, bathes the landscape in warm, soft light, enhancing the colors and textures. Capture the magical moments when the animals are bathed in this enchanting light, creating an ethereal and captivating ambiance in your images.

v. **Predators in Action:** The Masai Mara's high density of predators provides unparalleled opportunities to capture thrilling wildlife interactions. Observe and photograph lions hunting, cheetahs in pursuit, or leopards perched on trees. Document the intensity, speed, and stealth of these predators as they display their hunting prowess. These action-packed moments offer dynamic and compelling photographs that convey the raw power and beauty of nature.

vi. **Birdlife:** The Masai Mara boasts a rich birdlife with over 450 recorded species. From majestic raptors such as eagles and vultures to vibrant and colorful birds like lilac-breasted rollers and African fish eagles, the avian diversity provides ample opportunities for bird photography. Capture their intricate plumage, unique behaviors, and graceful flights, showcasing the feathered wonders of the Mara.

vii. **Cultural Portraits:** Beyond wildlife, the Maasai people offer captivating subjects for cultural portraits. Capture the vibrant colors of their traditional attire, the expressive faces, and the distinctive jewelry and adornments. Photograph Maasai warriors in their regalia, Maasai women engaging in daily activities, or candid moments that reveal the spirit and character of the Maasai community.

In the Masai Mara, every moment presents a photographic opportunity waiting to be captured. Whether you're a wildlife enthusiast, landscape lover, or interested in cultural photography, the Masai Mara's abundance of subjects and stunning natural beauty will inspire and challenge your creativity. So pack your camera gear, seize the moment, and create images that tell the story of this remarkable destination.

Birdwatching Haven

The Masai Mara boasts an impressive variety of bird species, making it a paradise for birdwatchers. From majestic raptors, such as eagles and vultures, to vibrant and elusive species like the lilac-breasted roller and the African fish eagle, the Mara offers a wealth of birding opportunities for enthusiasts of all levels. Here's more about why the Masai Mara is a paradise for birdwatchers:

i. **Rich Birdlife:** The Masai Mara boasts a remarkable bird species diversity, with over 450 recorded species. From large raptors soaring in the sky to tiny colorful songbirds hidden in the grass, the Mara's birdlife is a delight for birdwatching enthusiasts. Spotting and identifying a wide range of species is an exciting challenge that offers endless rewards.

ii. **Resident and Migratory Birds:** The Masai Mara is home to a plethora of resident bird species that can be spotted year-round. Additionally, it serves as an important stopover for numerous migratory birds, making it a birdwatching hotspot during specific seasons. Witness the arrival of migratory birds from Europe and Asia, adding to the already rich birdlife of the region.

iii. **Varied Habitats:** The Masai Mara's diverse habitats provide niches for a wide array of bird species. From open grasslands to riverine forests, from acacia woodlands to wetlands, each habitat supports a unique bird community. Explore these different ecosystems to encounter species that thrive in specific environments, adding depth and variety to your birdwatching experience.

iv. **Raptor Sightings:** The Mara is known for its impressive raptor population, making it an ideal destination for raptor enthusiasts. Spot majestic eagles, falcons, hawks, and vultures as they soar across the savannah in search of prey. Witness their hunting techniques, observe their aerial displays, and capture awe-inspiring images of these birds of prey in action.

v. **Specialized Bird Species:** The Masai Mara is home to several specialized bird species that are not found in many other places. The localized species include the Masai Ostrich, Jackson's Widowbird, Fischer's Lovebird, and the Rufous-bellied Heron, among others. Birdwatchers have the opportunity to spot and appreciate these unique and sometimes elusive avian treasures.

vi. **Birding Guides and Resources:** The availability of experienced birding guides and resources in the Masai Mara ensures that birdwatchers receive expert assistance during their excursions. These guides possess extensive knowledge of local bird species, their behavior, and their habitats. They can help you identify species, locate specific birds, and share interesting insights into their natural history.

vii. **Birdwatching Hotspots:** The Masai Mara offers several designated birdwatching hotspots within the reserve. Explore areas such as the Mara River, the marshy regions, and the acacia woodlands, which are known for their high bird activity. These hotspots attract a diverse range of species, allowing you to witness bird interactions, breeding behaviors, and courtship displays.

Whether you are a seasoned birder or a beginner, the Masai Mara provides an incredible birdwatching experience. From rare and endemic species to stunning displays of flight and behavior, the Mara's avian diversity will captivate and inspire you. So grab your binoculars, reference guides, and camera, and get ready to explore the vibrant birdlife that thrives in this remarkable ecosystem.

Stunning Landscapes

The Masai Mara's expansive grassy plains, dotted with acacia trees and rocky outcrops, create a visually stunning backdrop for your adventures. Whether it's the golden hues of the savannah, the rugged beauty of the kopjes, or the winding Mara River, the landscapes of the Masai Mara are a feast for the eyes. Here's more about the landscapes that make the Masai Mara a photographer's dream and a paradise for nature lovers:

i. **Vast Savannahs:** The Masai Mara is characterized by vast open grasslands that stretch as far as the eye can see. These expansive savannahs create a sense of endlessness and evoke a feeling of connection with the wild. The golden grasses sway in the wind, providing a picturesque backdrop for wildlife sightings and offering stunning opportunities for landscape photography.

ii. **Acacia-dotted Plains:** Scattered throughout the Masai Mara are iconic acacia trees, their elegant silhouettes adding a touch of drama and charm to the landscape. The acacias provide shade for resting animals, serve as perches for birds of prey, and create striking compositions against the vast sky. These iconic trees have become synonymous with the African savannah and are a hallmark of the Masai Mara's beauty.

iii.   **Rolling Hills and Escarpments:** The Masai Mara is not solely flat grassland; it also features rolling hills and dramatic escarpments that add texture and depth to the scenery. These hills and escarpments offer vantage points for breathtaking views, providing a panoramic perspective of the reserve. Capture the undulating landscapes, with their contrasting colors and gradients, as they extend into the distance.

iv.   **Mara River:** The Mara River is a focal point of the landscape, snaking its way through the reserve. This vital water source sustains a diverse array of wildlife and creates stunning photographic opportunities. Watch as animals navigate the river, capturing dramatic moments during the Great Migration river crossings or witnessing predator-prey interactions in this watery realm.

v.   **Wetlands and Swamps:** The Masai Mara is dotted with wetlands and swamps, adding a different dimension to its landscapes. These areas are havens for birdlife, amphibians, and other water-dependent species. Explore the unique ecosystems of the swamps and capture the reflections, lush vegetation, and intricate network of water channels that create an oasis within the vast savannah.

vi. **Sunrise and Sunset Spectacles:** The Masai Mara's expansive skies and unobstructed horizons provide the perfect canvas for stunning sunrise and sunset spectacles. The African sun casts a warm glow over the landscape, transforming it into a palette of golden hues. Witness the sun as it rises or sets on the horizon, bathing the savannah in a magical light that enhances the beauty of the land and creates an ethereal atmosphere.

vii. **Weather and Cloud Formations:** The ever-changing weather patterns in the Masai Mara contribute to its captivating landscapes. Storm clouds brewing on the horizon, dramatic lightning displays, or rainbows arching across the sky add drama and intrigue to your photographs. The interplay of light and shadow, coupled with the dynamic weather conditions, allows for truly unique and striking landscape compositions.

The stunning landscapes of the Masai Mara offer a diverse range of visual experiences, from vast open plains to rugged hills and serene waterways. Whether you're capturing the grandeur of the savannah, the majestic acacias, or the dynamic sky, each frame tells a story of the untamed beauty that characterizes the Masai Mara. So, immerse yourself in the landscape, let your creativity flow, and capture the breathtaking vistas that will leave you in awe of nature's artistry.

Conservation and Sustainability

By visiting the Masai Mara, you contribute to the conservation efforts in the region. Your tourism dollars support initiatives that protect wildlife, preserve habitats, and empower local communities. It's an opportunity to make a positive impact while enjoying an unforgettable travel experience. Here's more about the conservation efforts and sustainable practices that are being implemented in the Masai Mara:

i. **Wildlife Conservation:** The Masai Mara is dedicated to the conservation of its iconic wildlife species. Efforts are focused on protecting and preserving the habitats of animals such as lions, elephants, cheetahs, and wildebeests. Conservation organizations, local communities, and government agencies collaborate to combat poaching, implement anti-trafficking measures, and enforce strict wildlife protection laws.

ii. **Community Involvement:** The engagement and participation of local communities are vital to the success of conservation efforts in the Masai Mara. Conservation initiatives aim to empower and involve local communities in decision-making processes and provide them with alternative livelihood opportunities that are sustainable and aligned with conservation goals. This fosters a sense of ownership and responsibility for the natural resources, leading to more effective conservation outcomes.

iii. **Anti-Poaching Measures:** Poaching poses a significant threat to the Masai Mara's wildlife. Efforts are made to combat poaching through increased law enforcement, community-based monitoring systems, and the development of anti-poaching units. These measures help deter illegal activities, protect vulnerable species, and preserve the delicate ecological balance of the reserve.

iv. **Sustainable Tourism Practices:** The tourism industry in the Masai Mara has embraced sustainable practices to minimize its environmental impact. Lodges and camps implement eco-friendly measures such as solar power usage, water conservation, waste management, and sustainable building materials. Responsible tourism guidelines are promoted to minimize disturbance to wildlife, respect cultural sensitivities, and encourage visitors to leave only footprints behind.

v. **Research and Monitoring:** Ongoing research and monitoring programs play a crucial role in understanding the Masai Mara's ecosystems, wildlife behavior, and ecological dynamics. Scientific studies provide valuable insights into the region's biodiversity, habitat changes, and conservation challenges. This knowledge informs conservation strategies and helps ensure the sustainable management of the reserve.

vi. **Environmental Education:** Environmental education and awareness programs are conducted to engage visitors, local communities, and future generations in conservation efforts. Educational initiatives focus on teaching the importance of biodiversity, sustainable practices, and the role each individual can play in protecting the environment. By fostering a sense of environmental stewardship, these programs contribute to a more sustainable future for the Masai Mara.

vii. **Partnerships and Collaborations:** Collaboration among various stakeholders, including government bodies, conservation organizations, tourism operators, and local communities, is essential for successful conservation and sustainability initiatives. Partnerships facilitate the sharing of resources, knowledge, and expertise, resulting in more effective conservation strategies and a holistic approach to preserving the Masai Mara's natural heritage.

The commitment to conservation and sustainability in the Masai Mara ensures that future generations can continue to experience and appreciate its extraordinary beauty and wildlife. Through a combination of wildlife protection, community involvement, sustainable tourism practices, research, and education, the Masai Mara strives to maintain its ecological integrity while benefiting the local communities that depend on its resources. By embracing conservation and sustainability, the Masai Mara serves as a model for responsible tourism and environmental stewardship.

The Masai Mara is a place of unrivaled natural beauty and cultural significance. It offers an immersive and transformative experience that allows you to witness the wonders of the animal kingdom, connect with ancient traditions, and appreciate the delicate balance of our planet's ecosystems. A journey to the Masai Mara is not just a trip; it's a life-enriching adventure that will leave a lasting impression.

Things you should know before traveling to Masai Mara

Before embarking on your journey to the Masai Mara, it's important to familiarize yourself with some key information to ensure a smooth and enjoyable experience. Here are some essential things you should know before traveling to the Masai Mara:

- **Entry Requirements:** Check the entry requirements for Kenya and ensure that you have a valid passport with at least six months of validity remaining. Depending on your nationality, you may need to obtain a visa before your arrival or apply for one upon entry.

- **Best Time to Visit:** The Masai Mara is a year-round destination, but the timing of your visit can greatly impact your experience. The Great Migration typically takes place from July to October, attracting a large number of wildebeests and other animals to the area. However, the Masai Mara offers excellent wildlife sightings and pleasant weather throughout the year, so consider your preferences when choosing your travel dates.

- **Weather and Climate:** The Masai Mara experiences a semi-arid climate with two distinct seasons: the dry season and the wet season. The dry season, from June to October, offers cooler temperatures and clear skies, while the wet season, from November to May, brings occasional rain showers and greener landscapes. Pack accordingly, with lightweight and breathable clothing for warmer days and layering options for cooler mornings and evenings.

- **Health and Safety:** It's essential to take proper health precautions before traveling to the Masai Mara. Check with your healthcare provider about recommended vaccinations and ensure that you have adequate travel insurance that covers medical expenses. Take precautions against malaria by using insect repellents, wearing protective clothing, and taking antimalarial medication as advised. Also, be mindful of wildlife safety and follow the guidance of experienced guides while on safari.

- **Accommodation and Safari Options:** The Masai Mara offers a range of accommodation options, from luxury lodges to tented camps and budget-friendly campsites. Research and book your accommodation well in advance, especially during peak seasons. Additionally, decide on the type of safari experience you prefer—guided game drives, hot air balloon safaris, walking safaris, or a combination of activities—and make arrangements accordingly.

- **Cultural Sensitivity:** The Masai Mara is home to the Maasai people, who have a rich cultural heritage. Respect their traditions, customs, and way of life by dressing modestly and seeking permission before taking photographs of individuals. Engage in cultural activities and interactions with local communities in a respectful and responsible manner, contributing to their sustainable development through appropriate initiatives.

- **Packing Essentials:** When packing for your trip, consider essentials such as comfortable and breathable clothing suitable for safari activities, sturdy walking shoes or boots, a hat, sunglasses, sunscreen, insect repellent, a good camera with extra batteries and memory cards, binoculars for wildlife viewing, and a reusable water bottle to minimize plastic waste. Don't forget to pack any necessary medications and a basic first aid kit.

- **Respect for Wildlife and Environment:** While in the Masai Mara, it's crucial to respect the wildlife and their natural habitat. Maintain a safe distance from animals, follow your guide's instructions, and avoid disrupting their behavior or habitat. Dispose of waste properly and adhere to responsible tourism practices to minimize your impact on the environment.

- **Currency and Payment:** The official currency of Kenya is the Kenyan Shilling (KES). Credit cards are widely accepted in major establishments, but it's advisable to carry some cash for smaller purchases and tips. Ensure that you have enough local currency for gratuities, park fees, and any additional expenses that may not accept cards.

- **Communication and Connectivity:** While in the Masai Mara, be prepared for limited or no access to mobile networks and internet connectivity. Consider purchasing a local SIM card if you need communication during your stay. However, embrace the opportunity to disconnect and immerse yourself fully in the natural wonders of the reserve.

By keeping these important aspects in mind, you can better prepare for your trip to the Masai Mara and make the most of your experience. Remember to plan ahead, respect the environment and local culture, and embrace the beauty and wildlife encounters that await you in this remarkable destination.

Top Dos and Don'ts in Masai Mara

When visiting the majestic Masai Mara, it's important to be mindful of your actions to ensure a positive and responsible experience for both you and the environment. By following a set of top dos and don'ts, you can maximize your enjoyment while minimizing any negative impacts on the delicate ecosystem and local communities. Here are some essential guidelines to keep in mind during your visit to the Masai Mara:

Dos in Masai Mara

By following a set of dos, you can enhance your experience while promoting the conservation of wildlife, respecting local communities, and preserving the pristine environment of this iconic destination. Here are some key dos to keep in mind during your visit to the Masai Mara:

⊥ Respect Wildlife

Respecting wildlife is of utmost importance when visiting the Masai Mara. The region is renowned for its incredible biodiversity and iconic animal species. Here are some additional guidelines to further emphasize the importance of respecting wildlife:

i. **Maintain a Safe Distance:** It is crucial to maintain a safe distance from the wildlife to ensure both their safety and your own. Follow the instructions of experienced guides and park rangers who are knowledgeable about animal behavior and safety protocols. By keeping a respectful distance, you minimize the risk of disturbing or provoking the animals.

ii. **Avoid Feeding or Touching Animals:** Feeding wildlife can have severe consequences for their health and well-being. Human food is not part of their natural diet, and dependence on it can disrupt their natural feeding patterns and lead to health problems. Additionally, avoid the temptation to touch or interact with the animals, as it can be harmful to both you and the wildlife. Keep in mind that wild animals are just that—wild—and they should be observed from a safe distance without any physical contact.

iii. **Use Appropriate Photography Etiquette:** Photography is a wonderful way to capture the beauty of the Masai Mara, but it should be done responsibly. Respect the animals' space and behavior by not getting too close or causing them distress. Be mindful of using zoom lenses or binoculars to capture detailed shots without intruding on their natural habitat. Avoid using flash photography, as it can startle and disorientate animals, potentially causing harm.

iv. **Observe and Learn:** Take the time to observe and learn about the wildlife in their natural environment. Appreciate their behaviors, interactions, and unique adaptations. Use the opportunity to deepen your understanding of the delicate balance of ecosystems and the interconnectedness of all living creatures. By observing without interference, you gain a greater appreciation for the beauty and complexity of the natural world.

v. **Practice Responsible Game Drives:** When on a game drive, respect the guidelines and rules set by the park authorities. Stay on designated paths and roads to avoid damaging vegetation or disturbing wildlife. Be patient and allow animals to move freely without trying to force or block their path. Remember that the wildlife's well-being and conservation take precedence over any desire for a closer encounter.

vi. **Educate Others:** Spread awareness about the importance of wildlife conservation and responsible tourism practices. Encourage fellow travelers to respect wildlife, follow ethical guidelines, and make conscious choices that protect the animals and their habitats. By sharing knowledge and promoting responsible behavior, you can contribute to the preservation of the Masai Mara's extraordinary wildlife for future generations.

Respecting wildlife in the Masai Mara is not only crucial for the animals' well-being but also for the preservation of the delicate ecosystem as a whole. By adopting these practices, you can play a vital role in ensuring the long-term survival and protection of the remarkable wildlife that calls the Masai Mara home.

✚ Practice Responsible Photography

Practicing responsible photography is essential when visiting the Masai Mara. Capturing stunning images of the wildlife and landscapes can be a memorable part of your experience, but it's important to do so in a way that respects the animals, their habitats, and the local environment. Here are some additional guidelines for practicing responsible photography:

i. **Respect the Animals' Space:** Maintain a safe and respectful distance from the wildlife. Getting too close can disrupt their natural behavior and cause stress or harm. Use telephoto lenses or zoom capabilities to capture close-up shots without intruding on their personal space.

ii. **Observe without Disturbing:** Be patient and observe the animals without trying to influence their behavior. Avoid making sudden movements, loud noises, or using flash photography, as these can startle or distress the animals. Remember, their well-being and natural behavior should always take precedence over getting the perfect shot.

iii. **Minimize Intrusiveness:** Blend into the environment and minimize your impact as much as possible. Use muted colors in your clothing to avoid drawing unnecessary attention to yourself. Keep a low profile and avoid making sudden or disruptive movements that could alarm or distract the animals.

iv. **Capture Natural Behavior:** Aim to capture the animals in their natural state, engaging in their typical behaviors. These images often tell a more authentic and compelling story. Resist the temptation to manipulate the scene or provoke reactions from the animals for the sake of a better photo.

v. **Be Mindful of Timing and Lighting:** Take advantage of the best lighting conditions for photography, which are typically early morning and late afternoon when the light is soft and golden. This not only enhances the aesthetics of your images but also minimizes the disturbance caused by flash or artificial lighting.

vi. **Share Ethical and Educational Content:** When sharing your photographs, use your platform to educate and inspire others about the importance of wildlife conservation and responsible travel. Share information about the animals, their habitats, and the challenges they face, while promoting ethical behavior and respect for wildlife.

vii. **Support Conservation Efforts:** Consider contributing to local conservation initiatives or organizations that work towards protecting the wildlife and habitats of the Masai Mara. By supporting these efforts, you can help ensure the long-term survival and preservation of the area's extraordinary biodiversity.

Remember, responsible photography goes hand in hand with responsible tourism. By following these guidelines, you can capture stunning images while minimizing your impact and promoting the well-being and conservation of the Masai Mara's wildlife. Let your photographs serve as a testament to the beauty of nature and inspire others to protect and cherish it.

⫟ Support Local Communities

Supporting local communities is not only a way to enhance your travel experience in the Masai Mara but also a means of contributing to the sustainable development and well-being of the region. By engaging with and supporting local communities, you can foster cultural exchange, empower local residents, and create positive social and economic impacts. Here are some additional ways to support local communities during your visit to the Masai Mara:

i. **Purchase Locally Made Products:** Seek out opportunities to purchase locally made crafts, artwork, and souvenirs. By buying directly from local artisans and vendors, you support their livelihoods and help preserve traditional craftsmanship. These purchases also serve as meaningful reminders of your journey and provide economic benefits to the community.

ii.   **Participate in Community-based Tourism:** Look for community-based tourism initiatives that provide authentic and immersive experiences with the local Maasai communities. These initiatives often include guided tours, cultural performances, visits to traditional villages, and opportunities to learn about Maasai customs, traditions, and ways of life. By participating in these activities, you support local guides, artists, and entrepreneurs, helping to generate income and promote cultural preservation.

iii.   **Respect Local Customs and Traditions:** Familiarize yourself with the customs and traditions of the local communities and demonstrate respect during your interactions. Learn about appropriate behavior, greetings, and gestures. Engage in genuine conversations, ask questions, and listen attentively to the stories shared by community members. By showing respect, you create a positive and meaningful cultural exchange.

iv. **Contribute to Local Initiatives:** Research and identify local initiatives or projects focused on conservation, education, healthcare, or community development. Consider making a contribution, whether financial or through volunteer work, to support these efforts. This can include supporting schools, healthcare clinics, conservation organizations, or community-driven projects that address specific needs and aspirations of the local community.

v. **Choose Accommodations with Local Ownership:** Opt for accommodations that are locally owned and operated. This ensures that a significant portion of the revenue generated stays within the community, supporting local employment and fostering economic growth. Additionally, these accommodations often provide opportunities for cultural immersion and interaction with the local staff.

vi. **Eat and Drink Local:** Explore local cuisine by dining at locally owned restaurants or trying traditional Maasai dishes. By supporting local eateries, you contribute to the local economy and encourage the preservation of traditional culinary practices. This is also an excellent opportunity to savor the flavors of the region and experience the diverse culinary heritage.

vii. **Engage in Responsible Tourism:** Practice responsible tourism by being mindful of your impact on the environment, culture, and communities. Respect local resources, use water and energy sparingly, and dispose of waste properly. Seek out tour operators and guides who prioritize responsible practices and have a positive relationship with the local communities.

Remember, supporting local communities goes beyond financial contributions. It involves fostering genuine connections, respecting cultural diversity, and understanding the challenges and aspirations of the local people. By supporting local initiatives and engaging with the community, you can help preserve traditions, improve livelihoods, and create a more sustainable future for the people of the Masai Mara.

⊹ Adhere to Park Rules and Regulations

Adhering to park rules and regulations is crucial for ensuring a safe and responsible visit to the Masai Mara. The rules are in place to protect the wildlife, preserve the environment, and maintain the overall integrity of the park. By following these guidelines, you contribute to the conservation efforts and help maintain the natural beauty of the area. Here are some additional points to consider when adhering to park rules and regulations:

i. **Familiarize Yourself with the Rules:** Before your visit, familiarize yourself with the specific rules and regulations of the Masai Mara National Reserve. These can include guidelines on wildlife interaction, driving and parking, camping, waste disposal, and visitor conduct. Obtain the necessary permits or passes required for entry and activities within the park.

ii. **Stay on Designated Paths and Roads:** Stick to designated paths, trails, and roads when exploring the park. Straying off these designated areas can damage fragile ecosystems, disrupt wildlife habitats, and cause soil erosion. Respect barriers and signs indicating restricted or sensitive areas, as they are in place for the protection of the environment and wildlife.

iii. **Observe Speed Limits:** When driving within the park, adhere to the specified speed limits. Driving at a moderate speed allows for better wildlife observation, reduces the risk of accidents, and minimizes disturbance to animals. It also helps preserve the integrity of the park's road infrastructure.

iv. **Do Not Feed the Wildlife:** Feeding wildlife is strictly prohibited within the Masai Mara National Reserve. Human food is not a part of their natural diet and can have detrimental effects on their health and behavior. Feeding animals can also encourage dependency and alter their natural foraging patterns, leading to potential conflicts with humans.

v. **Practice Proper Waste Management:** Carry out any waste you generate during your visit and dispose of it properly. Use designated trash bins or take your waste with you to be properly disposed of outside the park. Avoid littering, as it can harm wildlife and degrade the park's natural beauty.

vi.   **Respect Quiet Zones and Peaceful Enjoyment:**
Some areas within the park may have designated
quiet zones or restrictions on noise. Respect these
areas to provide an undisturbed environment for
wildlife and for the enjoyment of other visitors
seeking peace and tranquility. Keep noise to a
minimum, particularly during game drives and
other wildlife-viewing activities.

vii.   **Follow Wildlife Viewing Etiquette:** When
observing wildlife, maintain a safe distance and
avoid disturbing their natural behavior. Use
binoculars or telephoto lenses to get closer views
without encroaching on their space. Be patient and
allow animals to move freely without attempting to
direct or provoke them for a better photo
opportunity.

viii. **Report Any Violations:** If you witness any
violations of park rules or witness behavior that
may be harmful to wildlife or the environment,

report it to the appropriate park authorities. Your timely reporting can help preserve the integrity of the park and protect its inhabitants.

By adhering to park rules and regulations, you contribute to the sustainable management and preservation of the Masai Mara National Reserve. Responsible visitor behavior ensures the continued protection of the park's unique wildlife and natural ecosystems, allowing future generations to enjoy its beauty and biodiversity.

✦ Embrace Cultural Immersion

Embracing cultural immersion during your visit to the Masai Mara is an enriching way to connect with the local community and gain a deeper understanding of the region's heritage. The Maasai people, the indigenous inhabitants of the area, have a rich cultural identity that spans centuries. Here are some additional points to consider when embracing cultural immersion in the Masai Mara:

i.   **Learn About Maasai Culture:** Take the time to learn about the traditions, customs, and way of life of the Maasai people. Engage in conversations with community members, listen to their stories, and ask questions respectfully. This can be done through organized cultural visits, interactions with local guides, or visits to traditional Maasai villages.

ii. **Respect Cultural Practices:** Show respect for the cultural practices of the Maasai people. Be aware of any cultural protocols or customs and adhere to them during your interactions. This may include greetings, dress codes, or guidelines on entering sacred or private areas. By respecting their culture, you create a positive and meaningful exchange.

iii. **Participate in Cultural Activities:** Seek opportunities to participate in cultural activities organized by the local community. This can include traditional dances, music performances, storytelling sessions, or craft demonstrations. By engaging in these activities, you support the preservation of cultural traditions and contribute to the livelihoods of the Maasai people.

iv. **Visit Community Projects and Cooperatives:** Explore community-run projects and cooperatives that showcase Maasai craftsmanship, art, and products. These initiatives often provide economic opportunities for the local community, empowering them through sustainable income generation. Purchasing handmade crafts or locally produced goods directly from the community supports their economic independence.

v. **Volunteer or Contribute to Community Initiatives:** Consider volunteering your time and skills to support community initiatives in the Masai Mara. This could involve participating in education programs, conservation projects, or healthcare initiatives. Check with local organizations or lodges for opportunities to contribute positively to the community during your visit.

vi. **Respect Privacy and Seek Permission:** When interacting with individuals or entering community spaces, respect their privacy and seek permission when appropriate. Always ask before taking photographs of community members or their properties, as cultural sensitivity and personal privacy vary among individuals.

vii. **Support Local Guides and Providers:** Engage local guides, tour operators, and accommodation providers who have a close connection with the local community. They can provide authentic insights and ensure that the benefits of tourism reach the local people. By supporting local businesses, you contribute to the economic growth and empowerment of the community.

viii. **Be Open and Curious:** Approach cultural immersion with an open mind and a genuine curiosity to learn. Be receptive to new experiences, perspectives, and ways of life. Engage in meaningful conversations and be willing to challenge your own preconceived notions. This openness fosters a more profound connection with the local community.

Embracing cultural immersion in the Masai Mara allows you to go beyond being a passive observer and become an active participant in the preservation of cultural heritage. By engaging with the local community, supporting their initiatives, and respecting their traditions, you create lasting memories and contribute positively to the sustainable development of the region.

Don'ts in Masai Mara

When visiting the majestic Masai Mara, it's essential to not only focus on the dos but also be aware of the don'ts.

These guidelines help ensure a respectful and responsible experience while preserving the natural environment, protecting wildlife, and maintaining the integrity of the Masai Mara National Reserve. Understanding and adhering to these don'ts will contribute to the long-term conservation efforts and help safeguard this extraordinary ecosystem for generations to come. Here are some important points to keep in mind to ensure a responsible and enjoyable visit to the Masai Mara.

✦ Don't Feed or Touch the Animals

One crucial rule when visiting the Masai Mara is to never feed or touch the animals. While it may be tempting to get closer to the wildlife or offer them food, it is important to remember that these are wild animals in their natural habitat. Here are some reasons why you should never feed or touch the animals:

i. **Disturbs Natural Behavior:** Feeding or touching the animals disrupts their natural behavior and can lead to dependency on human-provided food. This interferes with their ability to forage and hunt for themselves, which can have long-term negative consequences for their survival in the wild.

ii. **Alters Social Dynamics:** The introduction of human food can cause conflicts within animal groups, disrupt their social hierarchy, and lead to aggression or territorial disputes. Feeding one animal can create an unfair advantage over others and upset the delicate balance of the ecosystem.

iii. **Health Risks:** Human food is not suitable for wild animals, and feeding them can have serious health implications. It can lead to malnutrition, obesity, digestive problems, and dependency on an unnatural diet. Additionally, animals that become accustomed to human food may approach vehicles or people in search of more, putting themselves at risk of injury or even death.

iv. **Encourages Aggressive Behavior:** When animals associate humans with food, they can become more aggressive in their pursuit of it. This can lead to dangerous encounters and put both visitors and animals at risk. It is essential to maintain a safe distance and respect the animals' wild nature.

v. **Disease Transmission:** Feeding or touching wildlife increases the risk of disease transmission between humans and animals. Human food may contain bacteria or viruses that can be harmful to animals, and vice versa. It is crucial to minimize any direct contact to protect the health and well-being of both wildlife and visitors.

vi. **Legal Consequences:** Feeding or touching wildlife is often illegal in protected areas such as the Masai Mara National Reserve. Violating these regulations can result in fines, legal action, or even expulsion from the park. It is essential to respect the rules and guidelines set forth by park authorities to ensure the conservation of the wildlife and their natural behaviors.

Remember, the Masai Mara is a place where wildlife thrives in its natural state. It is our responsibility as visitors to respect their space, observe them from a safe distance, and appreciate their beauty without interfering with their lives. By not feeding or touching the animals, we contribute to their preservation and ensure a sustainable future for the Masai Mara's remarkable biodiversity.

+ Don't Litter or Pollute

Another important rule to follow when visiting the Masai Mara is to never litter or pollute the environment. The natural beauty of the Masai Mara is a result of its pristine ecosystems, and it is our responsibility to preserve and protect this fragile environment. Here are some reasons why you should never litter or pollute in the Masai Mara:

i. **Environmental Impact:** Littering and pollution have a detrimental effect on the ecosystems and wildlife of the Masai Mara. Plastics, chemicals, and other pollutants can contaminate the water sources, soil, and vegetation, leading to habitat degradation and loss of biodiversity. Animals can mistake litter for food or become entangled in it, resulting in injury or death.

ii. **Human-Wildlife Conflict:** Litter can attract scavengers and predators, altering their natural behavior and increasing the risk of human-wildlife conflict. Animals may associate humans with food sources, leading to potentially dangerous encounters. It is important to keep the environment free of litter to avoid attracting wildlife to areas where they may come into conflict with humans.

iii. **Aesthetics and Visitor Experience:** Litter and pollution detract from the natural beauty of the Masai Mara, impacting the visitor experience. It takes away from the serenity and authenticity of the environment and can diminish the enjoyment of other visitors. Keeping the park clean ensures that everyone can appreciate the breathtaking landscapes without visual and environmental distractions.

iv. **Water Contamination:** The Masai Mara is home to rivers and water bodies that support a diverse range of wildlife. Litter and pollution can contaminate these water sources, posing a threat to both animals and humans. Clean water is essential for the survival and well-being of all life in the park, and it is our responsibility to maintain its purity.

v. **Cultural Respect:** Littering and polluting the environment disrespect the cultural values of the local Maasai community who have coexisted with the land for generations. Their way of life is closely tied to the natural environment, and by keeping the Masai Mara clean, we show respect for their traditions and customs.

vi. **Legal Consequences:** Littering and polluting are often illegal within protected areas like the Masai Mara National Reserve. Violating these regulations can result in fines, legal consequences, or expulsion from the park. It is important to respect and abide by the rules set forth by park authorities to ensure the preservation of the environment and the well-being of the wildlife.

By committing to a litter-free and pollution-free visit, we contribute to the long-term conservation of the Masai Mara. Always carry a reusable water bottle and bags for your waste, and dispose of them properly in designated bins or take them with you when leaving the park. Leave no trace behind and leave the environment as you found it, or even better. Together, we can preserve the beauty and ecological integrity of the Masai Mara for future generations to enjoy.

♣ Don't Disturb Cultural Sites or Heritage

Respecting the cultural sites and heritage of the Masai Mara is essential during your visit. The region is rich in cultural significance, with historical sites and traditions that hold immense value to the local Maasai community. Here are some reasons why you should never disturb cultural sites or heritage in the Masai Mara:

i.   **Cultural Preservation:** Cultural sites and heritage are valuable links to the history, traditions, and identity of the local community. By not disturbing these sites, you contribute to the preservation and safeguarding of their cultural heritage. Respect for their customs and traditions ensures that future generations can continue to learn from and appreciate their rich history.

ii. **Spiritual and Sacred Places:** Many cultural sites in the Masai Mara hold spiritual and sacred significance to the Maasai people. These areas are considered sacred grounds, and any disturbance or disrespect can be deeply offensive and disruptive to their beliefs and practices. It is important to approach these sites with reverence and refrain from any actions that could desecrate or disrespect their sanctity.

iii. **Environmental Impact:** Cultural sites are often located within sensitive natural environments. Disturbing these sites can have adverse effects on the surrounding ecosystems and habitats. Actions such as littering, trampling on vegetation, or removing artifacts can disrupt the natural balance and cause irreparable damage to the environment.

iv. **Legal and Ethical Considerations:** Many cultural sites and heritage areas within the Masai Mara may be protected by local, national, or international laws. Disrupting or damaging these sites can have legal consequences and may result in fines or legal action. It is essential to research and understand the regulations and guidelines regarding cultural sites before your visit and adhere to them diligently.

v. **Cultural Sensitivity:** Showing respect for the cultural sites and heritage demonstrates cultural sensitivity and a genuine interest in understanding and appreciating the local community. It fosters positive interactions and relationships between visitors and the Maasai people, creating a mutually enriching experience for both parties.

vi. **Responsible Tourism:** Being a responsible tourist means considering the impact of your actions on the local community and their cultural heritage. By not disturbing cultural sites, you contribute to sustainable tourism practices that prioritize the preservation and promotion of local culture. Responsible tourism ensures that the benefits of tourism are shared with and support the well-being of the community.

When visiting the Masai Mara, take the time to learn about the cultural sites and heritage of the region. Engage with local guides or community members who can provide valuable insights and guidance. Remember to treat these sites with respect, observe any guidelines or restrictions, and appreciate their cultural and historical significance. By embracing a responsible and respectful approach, you can contribute to the preservation and celebration of the vibrant cultural heritage of the Masai Mara.

✦ Don't Wander Off or Go Unaccompanied

When visiting the Masai Mara, it is crucial to avoid wandering off or going unaccompanied in certain areas. The reserve is a vast and wild landscape, and venturing alone or outside designated areas can be dangerous for several reasons:

i. **Wild Animals:** The Masai Mara is home to a diverse array of wildlife, including large predators and herbivores. Wandering off or straying from designated paths can lead to unexpected encounters with these animals, posing serious risks to personal safety. It is best to stay within designated areas and follow the guidance of experienced guides who are well-versed in animal behavior and safety protocols.

ii.   **Getting Lost:** The Masai Mara is a vast wilderness, and its landscape can be challenging to navigate, particularly for those unfamiliar with the area. Going unaccompanied increases the likelihood of getting lost, leading to potential distress and putting yourself at risk. Always stay close to your guide or group to ensure your safety and avoid getting separated.

iii.   **Conservation and Preservation:** The Masai Mara is a protected area aimed at conserving its unique biodiversity. Wandering off can inadvertently disturb wildlife habitats, damage vegetation, and contribute to erosion. Staying within designated paths and zones helps minimize human impact and supports conservation efforts.

iv. **Respect for Local Customs:** The Masai Mara is also home to the Maasai community, and certain areas may hold cultural or spiritual significance. Wandering off into restricted areas can be disrespectful to the local customs and traditions. It is essential to be mindful of cultural sensitivities and adhere to the guidance of local guides and community members.

v. **Safety from Other Hazards:** In addition to wildlife, the Masai Mara terrain can present other potential hazards, such as uneven ground, hidden crevices, or water bodies. Staying with experienced guides ensures you avoid these dangers and have a safe and enjoyable experience.

vi. **Legal and Park Regulations:** Straying into unauthorized areas may violate park regulations and guidelines, leading to potential fines or penalties. Park authorities have established designated routes and rules for visitors to protect both people and wildlife.

To make the most of your visit to the Masai Mara while ensuring your safety, always stay with your designated guide or group. These experienced professionals are knowledgeable about the area, wildlife behavior, and potential risks. They will ensure that you have a rewarding and safe experience while respecting the environment, wildlife, and local customs. Following these guidelines helps contribute to the preservation of this extraordinary wilderness and the rich cultural heritage of the Masai Mara.

⊥ Don't Support Illegal Activities

When visiting the Masai Mara, it is vital to refrain from supporting or engaging in any illegal activities. Responsible tourism means respecting the laws and regulations in place to protect the environment, wildlife, and local communities. Here are some reasons why you should never support illegal activities in the Masai Mara:

i. **Conservation and Wildlife Protection:** Illegal activities such as poaching, wildlife trafficking, or trading in endangered species pose a significant threat to the conservation efforts in the Masai Mara. These activities exploit and harm the local wildlife populations, disrupt the natural balance of the ecosystem, and jeopardize the long-term survival of endangered species. By not supporting illegal activities, you contribute to the protection and preservation of the remarkable biodiversity of the region.

ii.   **Environmental Sustainability:** The Masai Mara's delicate ecosystems require careful stewardship and sustainable practices to maintain their health and resilience. Illegal activities such as illegal logging, bushmeat trade, or destructive fishing practices can degrade habitats, contribute to deforestation, and lead to soil erosion and water pollution. Supporting legal and sustainable activities helps promote environmental sustainability and the long-term well-being of the ecosystem.

iii. **Respect for Local Communities:** Illegal activities often exploit local communities, undermining their rights, livelihoods, and cultural heritage. Supporting legal and ethical practices ensures that the benefits of tourism are shared with the local communities and that their rights and interests are respected. It also encourages responsible and sustainable tourism practices that contribute positively to the social and economic development of the region.

iv. **Legal Consequences:** Engaging in or supporting illegal activities within the Masai Mara can have severe legal consequences. Authorities are committed to preserving the integrity of the reserve and combating illegal practices. Visitors found involved in illegal activities may face fines, legal action, or expulsion from the park. It is crucial to be aware of and abide by the laws and regulations governing the Masai Mara National Reserve.

v. **Ethical Responsibility:** As responsible travelers, it is our ethical responsibility to promote and support legal, sustainable, and ethical practices. By making informed choices, supporting licensed operators, and reporting any suspicious activities, you contribute to the overall well-being of the Masai Mara and help combat illegal activities.

vi. **Preservation of Cultural Heritage:** Illegal activities can also impact the cultural heritage of the Masai Mara, such as illegal excavations or looting of archaeological sites. These actions erode the historical and cultural significance of the region. Respecting and preserving the cultural heritage of the Masai Mara ensures that future generations can continue to learn from and appreciate the rich history and traditions of the local communities.

By actively choosing not to support illegal activities, you play a crucial role in protecting the environment, wildlife, and cultural heritage of the Masai Mara. Engage in responsible and ethical tourism practices, support licensed operators, report any illegal activities you witness, and contribute to the sustainable development and conservation of this extraordinary destination.

Adhering to this don'ts, you can contribute to the conservation efforts, respect the local culture, and ensure a sustainable and memorable experience in the Masai

Mara. Let your visit be a positive force for the preservation of this incredible ecosystem, so that future generations can continue to enjoy its wonders.

Plan your trip to Masai Mara

Planning a trip to the Masai Mara is an exciting endeavor that offers the opportunity to immerse yourself in the breathtaking beauty of the African wilderness. The Masai Mara National Reserve, located in southwestern Kenya, is renowned for its abundant wildlife, stunning landscapes, and vibrant cultural heritage. To make the most of your experience, proper planning is essential. From choosing the best time to visit to arranging accommodations and activities, careful preparation ensures a seamless and unforgettable journey. In this guide, we will explore the key steps to help you plan your trip to the Masai Mara, allowing you to create cherished memories while respecting the environment, wildlife, and local communities. Here are some key steps to help you plan your trip to the Masai Mara:

i.   **Determine the Best Time to Visit:** The Masai Mara offers different experiences throughout the year. The Great Migration, where vast herds of wildebeest and other animals migrate, usually takes place from July to October. However, the park is captivating year-round, with diverse wildlife and stunning landscapes. Consider your interests, weather preferences, and wildlife sightings when choosing your travel dates.

ii. **Research Entry Requirements:** Check the entry requirements for traveling to Kenya, including visa requirements, passport validity, and any health-related regulations. Ensure that you have all the necessary documentation in order to enter the country legally.

iii. **Choose the Right Accommodation:** The Masai Mara offers a range of accommodation options, including lodges, tented camps, and luxury resorts. Consider the level of comfort, proximity to wildlife, and your budget when selecting accommodation. Look for eco-friendly and community-focused properties that align with your values.

iv.   **Select a Reputable Tour Operator:** Working with a reputable tour operator is highly recommended for a well-organized and safe trip to the Masai Mara. They can arrange transportation, game drives, and other activities while providing valuable insights and guidance throughout your journey. Look for operators with extensive experience, positive reviews, and a commitment to sustainable tourism practices.

v.   **Plan Activities and Wildlife Viewing:** Research the activities you want to participate in and plan your wildlife viewing experiences accordingly. Game drives are a popular choice for spotting wildlife, but other activities like hot air balloon safaris, guided walks, and cultural visits can enhance your overall experience. Coordinate with your tour operator to create a well-rounded itinerary that matches your interests and priorities.

vi.   **Pack Accordingly:** Pack appropriate clothing for the weather and activities. Lightweight, breathable, and neutral-colored clothing is recommended for safari excursions. Don't forget essentials like comfortable shoes, a hat, sunscreen, insect repellent, and a good pair of binoculars. It's also advisable to pack any necessary medications, toiletries, and a reusable water bottle.

vii.   **Consider Travel Insurance:** It's advisable to obtain travel insurance that covers medical emergencies, trip cancellations, and any other unforeseen circumstances. This will provide you with peace of mind during your trip.

viii.   **Respect Local Customs and Wildlife:** Familiarize yourself with the local customs, traditions, and etiquette of the Maasai people and the park's regulations. Respect wildlife by maintaining a safe distance, not feeding or touching animals, and following responsible photography guidelines. By being mindful of local customs and wildlife conservation, you can contribute to the preservation of the Masai Mara's natural and cultural heritage.

ix. **Prepare for Connectivity and Services:** Keep in mind that connectivity and services in the Masai Mara may be limited. Check with your accommodation provider about the availability of amenities such as Wi-Fi, electricity, and mobile network coverage. Consider bringing portable chargers or extra batteries for your electronic devices.

x. **Stay Informed and Flexible:** Stay updated on any travel advisories, weather conditions, or changes in park regulations leading up to and during your trip. Be prepared for unexpected circumstances and maintain flexibility in your plans to accommodate any unforeseen events or opportunities that may arise.

By carefully planning your trip to the Masai Mara, you can maximize your enjoyment of this awe-inspiring destination. With the right preparations and a respectful approach, you will create lasting memories and contribute to the conservation of the incredible wildlife and cultural heritage of the Masai Mara.

Masai Mara tourist Visa requirements

If you're planning a trip to the breathtaking Masai Mara National Reserve in Kenya, it's important to understand the tourist visa requirements. Acquiring the appropriate visa will ensure a smooth entry into the country, allowing you to fully enjoy the wonders of the Masai Mara. In this guide, we will provide an introduction to the tourist visa requirements for visiting the Masai Mara, including the necessary documentation, application process, and important considerations. By familiarizing yourself with these requirements, you can embark on your journey to the Masai Mara with confidence and ease.

Types of Visas

When planning a visit to the Masai Mara in Kenya, it's essential to understand the different types of visas available for travelers. The type of visa you need will depend on the purpose and duration of your stay. Here are the common types of visas for visiting the Masai Mara:

i. **Tourist Visa:** The tourist visa is the most common type of visa for travelers visiting Kenya for leisure or tourism purposes, including a trip to the Masai Mara. It allows for a single entry into the country and is typically valid for up to 90 days. This visa is suitable for short-term visits and exploration of the national parks, including the Masai Mara National Reserve.

ii. **Multiple Entry Visa:** If you plan to leave and re-enter Kenya multiple times within a specified period, a multiple entry visa is required. This visa allows for multiple entries into the country during its validity. It is ideal for travelers who plan to visit neighboring countries or take side trips during their stay in Kenya.

iii. **Business Visa:** The business visa is intended for individuals traveling to Kenya for business-related purposes, such as attending conferences, meetings, or exploring potential business opportunities. It allows for a single entry and is typically valid for a short duration, ranging from a few days to a few months, depending on the specific requirements.

iv. **Transit Visa:** If you have a layover or transit through a Kenyan airport, you may need a transit visa. This visa permits you to stay in the country for a limited period while you wait for your onward flight. Transit visas are usually valid for a short duration, typically up to 72 hours, and are specific to travelers who do not intend to leave the airport premises.

v. **Diplomatic and Official Visas:** Diplomatic and official visas are issued to individuals traveling to Kenya on official government business or representing their countries in an official capacity. These visas are granted to diplomats, government officials, and individuals on diplomatic missions. The specific requirements and application process for diplomatic and official visas may differ from regular tourist visas.

It is important to note that visa regulations and requirements can vary based on your nationality. It is advisable to check with the Kenyan Embassy or Consulate in your home country or consult their official website for the most up-to-date information regarding visa types, requirements, and application procedures specific to your nationality. Remember to apply for the appropriate visa well in advance of your intended travel dates to allow for processing time. Ensure that you have all the necessary documentation, including a valid passport, passport-sized photographs, proof of travel itinerary, and any other supporting documents required for the specific visa type. By understanding the various types of visas available for visiting the Masai Mara, you can choose the most appropriate one for your travel needs and enjoy a seamless entry into Kenya to explore the wonders of the Masai Mara National Reserve.

Visa Application Process

The visa application process is an important step when planning a visit to the Masai Mara in Kenya. Understanding the application process and ensuring that you have all the necessary documents and information will help facilitate a smooth and successful visa application. Here are the general steps involved in the visa application process for visiting the Masai Mara:

i. **Determine the Visa Type:** Identify the specific type of visa required for your visit to the Masai Mara. This could be a tourist visa, multiple entry visa, business visa, or any other visa category that aligns with the purpose and duration of your stay. Visit the official website of the Kenyan Embassy or Consulate in your country to obtain accurate information regarding the specific visa requirements for your nationality.

ii. **Gather Required Documents:** Compile all the necessary documents needed for the visa application. Common documents typically include:

- **Valid passport:** Ensure that your passport is valid for at least six months beyond your intended departure date from Kenya. It should also have sufficient blank pages for the visa stamp.
- **Completed visa application form:** Fill out the application form accurately and completely. Some countries may require an online application, while others may have downloadable forms to be submitted in person or via mail.
- **Passport-sized photographs:** Provide recent photographs that meet the specified requirements (size, background, etc.).
- **Proof of travel itinerary:** Include details of your travel plans, such as flight bookings, accommodation reservations, and a

comprehensive itinerary for your visit to the Masai Mara.

- **Proof of financial means:** Provide evidence of sufficient funds to cover your expenses during your stay in Kenya. This may include bank statements, sponsorship letters, or other relevant financial documents.

- **Pay the Visa Fee:** Determine the applicable visa fee for your visa type and pay it according to the specified method outlined by the Kenyan Embassy or Consulate. Fees can vary depending on the visa category and nationality. Payment is typically made in local currency or as specified by the consulate.

iii. **Submit the Application:** Submit your completed application form, supporting documents, and visa fee payment to the appropriate Kenyan Embassy or Consulate. This can often be done in person, through mail, or electronically, depending on the consular services available in your country.

iv. **Application Processing:** Allow sufficient time for the visa application to be processed. The processing time can vary depending on the embassy or consulate and the volume of applications received. It is advisable to apply well in advance of your intended travel dates to account for any unforeseen delays.

v. **Passport Return:** Once the visa application is processed, your passport will be returned to you with the visa affixed, either as a stamp or a visa sticker. In some cases, you may need to collect your passport in person, while in others, it may be returned to you via mail or courier service.

vi. **Travel with Visa:** Ensure that you carry your passport with the visa when traveling to Kenya and present it upon arrival at the immigration checkpoint. The immigration officer will verify your visa and other travel documents before granting you entry into the country.

It is important to note that visa requirements, application procedures, and processing times can vary based on your nationality and the country where you submit your application. It is recommended to check the official website of the Kenyan Embassy or Consulate in your country or consult with the relevant authorities to obtain the most accurate and up-to-date information regarding the visa application process for visiting the Masai Mara.

By following the visa application process diligently and providing all the required documents, you can ensure a successful application and look forward to an amazing experience exploring the wonders of the Masai Mara in Kenya.

Passport Requirements

When planning a trip to the Masai Mara, it is crucial to understand the passport requirements to ensure a smooth entry into Kenya. Your passport is an essential travel document that verifies your identity and citizenship. Here are the key passport requirements to consider:

i. **Validity:** Ensure that your passport is valid for at least six months beyond your intended departure date from Kenya. Many countries, including Kenya, require this minimum validity period as a standard entry requirement. If your passport is set to expire soon, it is advisable to renew it before your trip.

ii. **Blank Pages:** Check that your passport has enough blank pages for entry and exit stamps. Some countries require at least two to four consecutive blank pages for immigration purposes. These pages allow immigration officials to affix the necessary stamps and endorsements upon your arrival and departure from Kenya.

iii. **Damage or Wear:** Inspect your passport for any signs of damage or wear. Passports that are significantly torn, damaged, or illegible may be deemed invalid and could lead to complications during the entry process. It is best to have a passport in good condition to avoid any issues.

iv. **Additional Entry Requirements:** Apart from passport validity, Kenya may have additional entry requirements specific to certain nationalities. This could include visa requirements, vaccination certificates (such as yellow fever), or other supporting documents. Check with the Kenyan Embassy or Consulate in your country to determine if there are any additional requirements for your nationality.

v.   **Photocopies or Digital Copies:** It is advisable to carry photocopies or digital copies of your passport's main page and relevant visa pages. These copies can be useful in case of loss or theft, as they provide proof of identity and can assist in obtaining a replacement passport at the nearest embassy or consulate.

vi.   **Passport Security:** Safeguard your passport throughout your trip. Keep it in a secure place, such as a hotel safe, when not needed for identification purposes. Be mindful of pickpockets and take precautions to prevent theft or loss. Losing your passport can result in significant delays and complications, so it is essential to protect it at all times.

Remember to verify the passport requirements specific to your country of citizenship and consult the official website of the Kenyan Embassy or Consulate for the most up-to-date and accurate information. Adhering to these passport requirements ensures a smooth entry into Kenya and allows you to fully enjoy your visit to the extraordinary Masai Mara.

Yellow Fever Vaccination Certificate

When planning a trip to the Masai Mara in Kenya, it's important to be aware of the yellow fever vaccination certificate requirement. Yellow fever is a viral disease transmitted by infected mosquitoes and is prevalent in certain regions of Africa, including Kenya. Here's what you need to know about the yellow fever vaccination certificate:

i.   **Mandatory Requirement:** Kenya requires proof of yellow fever vaccination if you are arriving from or have transited through countries with a risk of yellow fever transmission. This requirement aims to protect both travelers and the local population from the spread of the disease.

ii.   **Validity Period:** The yellow fever vaccination certificate is generally considered valid for life. However, some countries and airlines may require a booster dose after a specific number of years. It is recommended to check the requirements of your home country and the airline you are traveling with regarding the validity period.

iii.   **Obtaining the Vaccine:** Yellow fever vaccination can be obtained at authorized vaccination centers or clinics designated by your country's health department. Make sure to receive the vaccine at least ten days before your departure to allow for the development of immunity.

iv.   **International Certificate of Vaccination:** Once you receive the yellow fever vaccine, you will be issued an International Certificate of Vaccination or Prophylaxis (ICVP). This certificate must be completed by the administering healthcare professional and includes information such as the date of vaccination and the vaccine's batch number.

v.   **Presentation at Immigration:** Upon arrival in Kenya, you will need to present your valid yellow fever vaccination certificate to immigration officials. They will verify that you have been vaccinated against yellow fever and that your certificate meets the necessary requirements.

vi.   **Keep the Certificate Safe:** It is important to keep your yellow fever vaccination certificate safe throughout your journey. Make multiple copies and store them separately in case the original is lost or damaged. Additionally, keep the original certificate with your travel documents to present it when required.

vii.   **Other Vaccinations:** While yellow fever is the primary vaccination requirement for Kenya, it is advisable to check if there are any other recommended vaccinations for your visit to the Masai Mara. This may include vaccines for diseases like typhoid, hepatitis A and B, tetanus, and others. Consult with a healthcare professional or travel clinic for personalized advice based on your medical history and travel plans.

Complying with the yellow fever vaccination certificate requirement is essential to ensure a smooth entry into Kenya and protect public health. Failure to present a valid certificate may result in denial of entry or quarantine measures. Make sure to check the yellow fever vaccination requirements well in advance of your trip and make the necessary arrangements to obtain the vaccine if needed. By doing so, you can enjoy your visit to the Masai Mara without any health-related concerns.

Visa-on-Arrival

Visa-on-Arrival (VoA) is an option available for certain nationalities visiting Kenya, including those planning to explore the wonders of the Masai Mara. With a Visa-on-Arrival, travelers can obtain their visa upon arrival at the Kenyan airport or border crossing point. Here's what you need to know about the Visa-on-Arrival process:

i. **Eligible Nationalities:** The Visa-on-Arrival option is available for citizens of specific countries determined by the Kenyan government. It is essential to check if your country of citizenship is eligible for this type of visa. You can find the list of eligible countries on the official website of the Kenyan Embassy or Consulate in your home country.

ii. **Purpose of Visit:** Visa-on-Arrival is typically granted for tourism, business, or medical purposes. Ensure that your visit falls within one of these categories to be eligible for this type of visa.

iii. **Requirements:**

- **Valid Passport:** Ensure that your passport is valid for at least six months beyond your intended departure date from Kenya.

- **Supporting Documents:** Prepare any supporting documents required for the visa application, such as proof of travel itinerary, accommodation details, return flight tickets, or invitation letters for business purposes. The specific requirements may vary, so check with the Kenyan Embassy or Consulate in your country for the precise documentation needed.

- **Visa Fee:** Be prepared to pay the visa fee in cash (usually in US dollars) upon arrival. The fee may vary based on your nationality and the type of visa required.

- **Yellow Fever Vaccination Certificate:** If your country is on the list of yellow fever risk countries, you may need to present a valid yellow fever vaccination certificate upon arrival.

iv. **Application Process:**

- Upon arrival at the Kenyan airport or border crossing point, proceed to the designated Visa-on-Arrival counter.
- Complete the visa application form, which is typically provided at the airport.
- Submit the application form, your passport, supporting documents, and the visa fee to the immigration officer.
- The immigration officer will review your documents and process your visa application.

- Once approved, the visa sticker or stamp will be affixed to your passport, granting you permission to enter Kenya.

v. **Validity and Duration:** The validity and duration of the Visa-on-Arrival can vary depending on your specific circumstances, purpose of visit, and the discretion of the immigration officer. It is crucial to check the details provided by the immigration officer to understand the terms of your visa.

vi. **Extension:** If you wish to extend your stay in Kenya beyond the validity of your Visa-on-Arrival, you can apply for an extension at the Immigration Office in Nairobi or other designated immigration offices. It is advisable to apply for an extension before your visa expires to avoid any immigration complications.

It's important to note that the availability and requirements of Visa-on-Arrival can change. Therefore, it is highly recommended to check the official website of the Kenyan Embassy or Consulate in your home country for the most up-to-date and accurate information regarding Visa-on-Arrival eligibility and procedures.

Visa-on-Arrival provides a convenient option for eligible travelers to obtain their visa upon arrival in Kenya, allowing them to embark on their journey to explore the wonders of the Masai Mara without the need for prior visa arrangements.

Visa Extensions

If you wish to extend your stay in Kenya, including your visit to the Masai Mara, beyond the validity of your initial visa, you can apply for a visa extension. Here's what you need to know about the visa extension process:

i. **Timing**: It is advisable to apply for a visa extension before your current visa expires. Plan ahead and initiate the extension process well in advance to allow sufficient time for processing and avoid any immigration complications.

ii. **Extension Eligibility:** Visa extensions are typically granted for valid reasons such as tourism, business, medical treatment, or other approved purposes. Ensure that your reason for extension falls within the accepted categories and provide appropriate documentation to support your application.

iii. **Application Procedure:**

- **Obtain the visa extension application form:** Visit the nearest Immigration Office in Kenya or check the official website of the Department of Immigration for the application form. Alternatively, some

Immigration Offices may offer online submission options.

- **Complete the application form:** Fill out the form accurately and provide all the necessary details, including your current visa information, purpose of extension, and intended duration of stay.

- **Gather supporting documents:** Prepare the required supporting documents, which may include a valid passport, copies of your current visa and entry stamp, proof of travel itinerary, financial means to support your extended stay, and any other relevant documents based on the purpose of your extension.

- **Submit the application:** Submit your completed application form and supporting documents to the Immigration Office in

Kenya. Ensure that you provide all the required information and meet the application submission requirements specified by the immigration authorities.

- **Pay the fee:** Pay the visa extension fee as per the regulations and guidelines provided by the Immigration Office. The fee amount may vary depending on the type of extension and duration requested.

- **Await the decision:** The immigration authorities will review your application, verify the supporting documents, and make a decision regarding your visa extension. The processing time can vary, so it's advisable to follow up with the Immigration Office or check their website for updates on the status of your application.

iv. **Compliance with Regulations:** During the visa extension period, it is important to continue adhering to the laws, regulations, and conditions of your visa. Abiding by these rules ensures your legal status in the country and prevents any potential penalties or complications.

v. **Departure Planning:** If you plan to depart Kenya before your visa extension application is processed, ensure that you have sufficient time left on your initial visa to cover your stay. Departing the country before the expiration of your initial visa is important to avoid any potential overstay issues.

It is essential to note that visa extension processes and requirements can vary, and the decision to grant an extension lies with the immigration authorities. It is recommended to consult with the Immigration Office or seek advice from an immigration lawyer or professional to ensure accurate and up-to-date information for your specific circumstances. By following the proper procedures and submitting the necessary documents, you can extend your stay in Kenya, including your visit to the Masai Mara, and continue to explore the natural wonders and cultural heritage of this remarkable destination.

Consult with the Kenyan Embassy/Consulate

Consulting with the Kenyan Embassy or Consulate in your home country is an essential step when planning a trip to the Masai Mara in Kenya. The embassy or consulate can provide valuable information and guidance regarding visa requirements, entry regulations, and other important details specific to your nationality. Here's why it's important to consult with the Kenyan Embassy or Consulate:

i.   **Accurate and Up-to-Date Information:** The Kenyan Embassy or Consulate is the official representation of Kenya in your home country. They are equipped with the most accurate and up-to-date information regarding visa requirements, application processes, entry regulations, and other essential details for travelers. By consulting with them, you can obtain the most reliable information to plan your trip accordingly.

ii. **Specific Requirements for Your Nationality:** Visa requirements and entry regulations can vary depending on your nationality. The Kenyan Embassy or Consulate can provide you with the specific requirements based on your citizenship. They can inform you about the visa types available, any additional documents needed, and any special considerations or restrictions that apply to your country of origin.

iii. **Application Procedures:** The embassy or consulate can guide you through the visa application process and provide details about the required documentation, application forms, fees, and submission methods. They can clarify any questions you may have regarding the application process, helping to ensure that you submit a complete and accurate application.

iv. **Clarification of Entry Regulations:** The Kenyan Embassy or Consulate can inform you about the entry regulations for Kenya, including any customs restrictions, health requirements, or travel advisories that may be in place. This information is important to ensure a smooth entry into Kenya and compliance with local laws and regulations.

v. **Consular Assistance:** In case of emergencies or unforeseen circumstances during your trip, the Kenyan Embassy or Consulate can provide consular assistance and support. They can assist with issues such as lost passports, emergency travel documents, or contacting family members in case of an emergency.

vi. **Travel Alerts and Updates:** The embassy or consulate can provide you with travel alerts, updates, or advisories related to your trip. They can inform you about any significant developments, such as changes in visa requirements, security situations, or natural disasters, that may affect your travel plans.

vii. **Cultural and Etiquette Guidance:** The Kenyan Embassy or Consulate can provide cultural and etiquette guidance, helping you understand local customs, traditions, and appropriate behavior during your visit to the Masai Mara. This information can enhance your cultural immersion and ensure respectful interactions with local communities.

It is advisable to contact the Kenyan Embassy or Consulate in your home country well in advance of your trip. They can provide you with the necessary information and answer any questions you may have, ensuring that you have a comprehensive understanding of the requirements and procedures for your visit to the Masai Mara.

By understanding the tourist visa requirements for visiting the Masai Mara, you can ensure a hassle-free entry into Kenya and fully immerse yourself in the wonders of this magnificent destination. Remember to check the visa requirements well in advance, gather the necessary documents, and complete the application process to embark on your extraordinary journey to the Masai Mara.

Program for Visa waiver

A visa waiver program allows travelers from certain countries to visit a destination without the need for a traditional visa. While Kenya currently does not have a visa waiver program in place, it is essential to stay updated on any changes in visa policies and regulations. However, many countries have implemented visa waiver programs with other nations, enabling their citizens to travel without a visa or with simplified visa procedures. Here's an overview of a typical visa waiver program:

i.   **Eligible Countries:** A visa waiver program identifies specific countries whose citizens are eligible for visa-free entry or simplified visa procedures. The selection of these countries is based on various factors, such as diplomatic relations, mutual agreements, economic ties, or regional considerations.

ii. **Reciprocity:** Visa waiver programs often operate on the principle of reciprocity, meaning that the participating countries grant visa-free entry to each other's citizens. This encourages bilateral travel and strengthens diplomatic relations between the nations involved.

iii. **Duration of Stay:** Visa waiver programs typically define the maximum duration of stay allowed for visa-free entry. This could range from a few days to several months, depending on the agreement between the participating countries.

iv. **Purpose of Visit:** The purpose of travel under a visa waiver program is usually limited to tourism, business meetings, or short-term visits. Any other activities, such as employment or long-term stays, may require a separate visa or permit.

v. **Entry Requirements:** While visa-free entry is granted under a waiver program, travelers are still subject to certain entry requirements. These may include possessing a valid passport with a specified minimum validity, proof of sufficient funds for the duration of the stay, return or onward tickets, and a clean criminal record.

vi. **Immigration Control:** Upon arrival, travelers may need to go through immigration control and present their valid passport to the immigration officers. The officers have the authority to deny entry if the traveler does not meet the entry requirements or poses a security risk.

It's important to note that a visa waiver program is a bilateral agreement between countries, and participation is determined by the governments involved. Therefore, if you are planning to visit Kenya, it is advisable to check with the Kenyan Embassy or Consulate in your home country to inquire about the current visa requirements and any updates on visa waiver programs that may be implemented in the future.

While a visa waiver program for Kenya is not currently in place, the Kenyan government may periodically review its visa policies to facilitate easier travel for eligible visitors. Stay informed and monitor official sources for any updates or changes to visa requirements to ensure a smooth travel experience to the extraordinary Masai Mara and other destinations in Kenya.

When is the best time to visit Masai Mara?

The best time to visit the Masai Mara depends on your specific interests and what you hope to experience during your trip. Here's a breakdown of the different seasons and their highlights to help you decide the best time for your visit:

i. **Great Migration (July to October):** One of the most iconic wildlife spectacles, the Great Migration, typically occurs between July and October in the Masai Mara. During this time, millions of wildebeest, zebras, and other herbivores cross the Mara River in search of fresh grazing. Witnessing this dramatic event is an extraordinary experience and a major draw for many visitors.

ii. **Dry Season (June to October):** The dry season is considered an excellent time for wildlife viewing in the Masai Mara. With less vegetation and limited water sources, animals tend to gather around waterholes and rivers, increasing the likelihood of spotting them. Predators such as lions, cheetahs, and leopards are also more active during this time as they take advantage of the high concentration of prey.

iii. **Calving Season (January to February):** The calving season, occurring around January and February, is another remarkable time to visit the Masai Mara. During this period, the wildebeest give birth to their young, attracting predators and creating a dynamic environment. It's a unique opportunity to witness the interactions between predators and their prey, as well as the vulnerability and resilience of the newborn animals.

iv. **Green Season (November to May):** The green season, also known as the rainy season, occurs from November to May. While the rains may bring lush vegetation and beautiful landscapes, wildlife viewing can be more challenging due to the increased foliage. However, the green season offers the opportunity to see migratory birds, newborn animals, and fewer crowds compared to the peak tourist season.

v. **Birdwatching (Year-round):** The Masai Mara is a haven for birdwatchers, with over 450 bird species recorded. Birdwatching enthusiasts can visit throughout the year, but the rainy season (November to May) is particularly rewarding as it attracts migratory bird species.

It's important to note that wildlife movements and weather patterns can vary each year, so there can be some variation in animal behavior and migration timing. It's always a good idea to consult with local guides, tour operators, or research current wildlife updates to get the latest information on animal sightings and movements.

Ultimately, the best time to visit the Masai Mara depends on your specific interests, whether it's witnessing the

Great Migration, observing predator-prey interactions, or experiencing the beauty of the landscapes. Each season offers unique opportunities, and any time of the year can be an extraordinary experience in the remarkable Masai Mara.

When to avoid visiting Masai Mara?

While the Masai Mara is a captivating destination with remarkable wildlife and landscapes, there are certain periods when visiting may not be ideal due to various factors. Here are some times to consider avoiding a visit to the Masai Mara:

i. **Rainy Season:** The rainy season in the Masai Mara occurs from November to May, with April and May typically being the wettest months. While the rain brings lush vegetation and beautiful landscapes, it can make wildlife viewing more challenging as animals disperse over larger areas and the thick foliage can obstruct views. Additionally, heavy rains can result in muddy roads, making transportation difficult.

ii. **Peak of the Long Rains:** The peak of the long rains, usually in April and May, can bring prolonged and heavy rainfall, which may lead to flooded areas and limited accessibility to certain parts of the park. It's advisable to avoid this period if you prefer dry and easier travel conditions.

iii. **High Season Crowds:** The peak tourist season in the Masai Mara, particularly during the Great Migration from July to October, attracts large numbers of visitors. While it's an incredible time to witness the migration, the park can get crowded, and accommodations and safari activities may be in high demand. If you prefer a more secluded and serene experience, you may want to avoid visiting during this time or plan your visit outside of the peak months.

iv. **Heatwaves:** The Masai Mara can experience high temperatures, especially during the months of January to March. Heatwaves can make the days uncomfortably hot, particularly for those who are not accustomed to high temperatures. If you are sensitive to heat, you may want to consider visiting during the cooler months or planning your activities for the cooler early mornings and late afternoons.

v. **Major Holidays and Events:** Consider avoiding major Kenyan holidays and events if you prefer fewer crowds and better availability of accommodations and services. National holidays like Christmas, Easter, and New Year's can be busy periods, with increased local and international visitors.

It's important to note that even during less ideal times to visit, the Masai Mara still offers incredible wildlife and scenic beauty. Wildlife can be spotted year-round, and each season brings its own unique experiences. Additionally, weather patterns and animal behavior can vary, so it's a good idea to consult with local guides or tour operators who can provide the latest updates on wildlife sightings and conditions.

By considering these factors and planning your visit accordingly, you can optimize your experience in the

Masai Mara and make the most of your time in this remarkable destination.

How to get to Masai Mara?

Getting to the Masai Mara involves traveling to Kenya and then making your way to the reserve itself. Here are the primary methods of transportation to reach the Masai Mara:

By Air:

- **International Flight:** If you are traveling from outside of Kenya, the first step is to book an international flight to Jomo Kenyatta International Airport (NBO) in Nairobi, the capital city of Kenya.

- **Domestic Flight:** From Nairobi, you can take a domestic flight to one of the airstrips located near the Masai Mara. The most common airstrips are Keekorok, Musiara, Olkiombo, and Mara Serena. Domestic airlines such as Safarilink, AirKenya, and Fly540 offer regular flights to these airstrips.

By Road:

- **Private Vehicle:** If you prefer a road trip, you can hire a private vehicle or a 4x4 safari vehicle in Nairobi and drive to the Masai Mara. The drive takes approximately 5-6 hours, depending on road conditions and traffic.

- **Shared or Organized Safari:** Another option is to join a shared or organized safari tour that includes transportation from Nairobi to the Masai Mara. These tours typically provide transportation in comfortable safari vehicles and may include other services such as accommodation, meals, and game drives.

Combination of Air and Road: Some travelers choose to combine air and road transportation for their journey to the Masai Mara. They fly from

Nairobi to one of the airstrips near the reserve and then continue their safari experience with a game drive or transfer by road to their lodge or camp within the Masai Mara.

It's important to plan your transportation in advance and consider factors such as cost, convenience, and the level of comfort you prefer. If you are booking a safari package, transportation arrangements may already be included. Otherwise, it's recommended to book flights or arrange for transportation with a reputable tour operator or travel agency that specializes in Kenya safaris.

Once you arrive in the Masai Mara, your chosen accommodation or safari operator will arrange for transfers to your lodge or camp within the reserve. Internal transportation within the Masai Mara is typically provided by safari vehicles operated by the lodges or safari companies.

By choosing the transportation method that suits your preferences and needs, you can embark on a memorable journey to the Masai Mara and immerse yourself in the breathtaking wildlife and natural beauty of this extraordinary destination.

Monthly breakdown of the best time to visit Masai Mara with activities

Planning a visit to the Masai Mara involves choosing the best time of year that aligns with your interests and desired activities. Each month in the Masai Mara offers unique experiences and wildlife sightings. To help you make an informed decision, here's a monthly breakdown of the best time to visit the Masai Mara, along with the activities you can enjoy during each period:

January

January is an exciting time to visit the Masai Mara, one of Africa's premier wildlife destinations. As the first month of the year, it brings fresh opportunities to witness incredible wildlife encounters and immerse yourself in the natural beauty of this remarkable ecosystem. From the calving season that kicks off the year to the pleasant weather, January offers a captivating experience for travelers seeking a safari adventure. Whether you're a wildlife enthusiast, a birdwatching enthusiast, or a cultural explorer, the Masai Mara in January has something extraordinary to offer. We will delve into the weather conditions, wildlife highlights, and activities that make January a fantastic time to explore the wonders of the Masai Mara. Get ready to embark on an unforgettable journey into the heart of the African wilderness as we discover the marvels of the Masai Mara in January. Here's a detailed overview of what you can expect during this month:

i.   **Weather:** In January, the weather in the Masai Mara is warm and pleasant, with average daytime temperatures ranging from 25°C to 30°C (77°F to 86°F). The nights can be slightly cooler, averaging around 15°C to 20°C (59°F to 68°F). Rainfall during this period is minimal, offering clear skies and plenty of sunshine.

ii. **Wildlife Highlights:** January marks the beginning of the calving season in the Masai Mara, making it an exciting time to visit. The wildebeest and other herbivores start giving birth to their young, attracting predators such as lions, cheetahs, and hyenas. Witnessing the newborn animals taking their first steps and observing the predator-prey interactions is a remarkable experience.

iii. **Activities:**

- **Wildlife Safaris:** Game drives during January provide excellent opportunities to spot a wide range of wildlife. Apart from the newborn animals, you can also see elephants, giraffes, zebras, buffalo, hippos, and numerous bird species.

- **Birdwatching:** January is a fantastic time for birdwatching in the Masai Mara. The resident and migratory bird populations are abundant, offering a diverse array of species to observe and photograph.

- **Cultural Interactions:** Engage in cultural experiences with the Maasai community to learn about their traditions, lifestyle, and conservation efforts. You can visit Maasai villages, participate in traditional ceremonies, and even go on guided nature walks with Maasai warriors.

- **Photography:** The beautiful lighting conditions, stunning landscapes, and unique wildlife interactions during the calving season make January an excellent time for wildlife photography in the Masai Mara.

Tips:

- Due to the pleasant weather and wildlife sightings, January can be a relatively busy time in the Masai Mara. It's advisable to book accommodations and safaris in advance to secure your preferred options.
- Pack lightweight and breathable clothing, as the daytime temperatures can be warm. However, it's

also a good idea to bring a light jacket or sweater for the cooler evenings.

- Don't forget essentials such as sunscreen, insect repellent, and a hat to protect yourself from the sun during game drives and outdoor activities.

January offers a unique opportunity to witness the circle of life in the Masai Mara with the arrival of newborn animals. Whether you're a wildlife enthusiast, a nature photographer, or someone seeking cultural immersion, this month provides an incredible experience that will leave you with unforgettable memories of the Masai Mara.

February

February marks a continuation of the calving season in the Masai Mara, a period of new beginnings and intense predator-prey interactions. The landscape is adorned with vibrant greenery, providing a stunning backdrop for thrilling wildlife sightings. Whether you're a nature enthusiast, a photography enthusiast, or simply seeking an immersive safari experience, February offers an array of opportunities to connect with the remarkable wildlife and cultural heritage of the Masai Mara.

i. **Weather:** During February, the Masai Mara experiences warm temperatures, creating a comfortable climate for exploration. Average daytime temperatures range from 25°C to 30°C (77°F to 86°F), making it an ideal time for outdoor activities. The evenings bring slightly cooler temperatures of around 15°C to 20°C (59°F to 68°F), allowing for a pleasant atmosphere to relax and enjoy the wilderness.

ii. **Wildlife Highlights:** The calving season is still in full swing during February, attracting predators such as lions, cheetahs, and hyenas. Witnessing the newborn animals taking their first steps and observing the dynamic predator-prey interactions is a captivating experience. You may have the opportunity to see wildebeest, zebras, and other herbivores crossing the plains, creating thrilling wildlife spectacles.

Activities:

- **Game Drives:** Embark on game drives through the vast savannahs of the Masai Mara, accompanied by experienced guides. Explore different areas of the reserve, increasing your chances of encountering a diverse range of wildlife.

- **Birdwatching:** February offers fantastic birdwatching opportunities, as migratory bird species join the resident bird population. Keep your binoculars ready to spot a variety of colorful birds, including raptors, waterbirds, and many other species.

- **Photography:** With the lush greenery and vibrant wildlife scenes, February provides ideal conditions for wildlife photography. Capture stunning moments of newborn animals, predators on the prowl, and the picturesque landscapes of the Masai Mara.

- **Cultural Interactions:** Engage with the local Maasai community to gain insights into their traditional way of life and cultural practices. Visit Maasai villages, interact with Maasai warriors, and learn about their conservation efforts and coexistence with wildlife.

Tips:

- Pack light, breathable clothing suitable for warm temperatures during the day. Layering options are recommended for cooler mornings and evenings.

- Don't forget to bring sun protection, including sunscreen, a hat, and sunglasses, as the African sun can be strong even in February.
- Carry a good pair of binoculars and a camera with telephoto lenses to capture the intricate details of wildlife encounters and bird species.

In February, the Masai Mara radiates with the joys of the calving season, creating an ambiance of new life and wildlife drama. With favorable weather and captivating wildlife sightings, this is a fantastic time to explore the natural wonders of the Masai Mara. Get ready to embark on an unforgettable safari adventure and create lasting memories in this iconic African wilderness.

March

March falls within the transition from the short dry season to the long rainy season in the Masai Mara. It is a time of change and renewal, with bursts of rainfall rejuvenating the landscape. The lush greenery, combined with the thriving wildlife, provides a picturesque backdrop for unforgettable safari experiences. Whether you are a nature enthusiast, a birdwatching enthusiast, or a cultural explorer, March offers a tapestry of opportunities to immerse yourself in the wonders of the Masai Mara.

i. **Weather:** During March, the Masai Mara experiences a mix of warm temperatures and occasional rainfall. Daytime temperatures typically range from 25°C to 30°C (77°F to 86°F), providing comfortable conditions for outdoor activities. However, it's essential to be prepared for intermittent showers, as the long rainy season gradually takes hold.

ii. **Wildlife Highlights:** While March marks the beginning of the long rainy season, wildlife sightings in the Masai Mara remain excellent. The rains replenish water sources, leading to increased wildlife activity. You can witness the interaction between predators and prey as they navigate the changing landscape. Lions, cheetahs, and other predators become more active, taking advantage of the abundance of herbivores.

Activities:

- **Game Drives:** Embark on game drives in search of the diverse wildlife species that inhabit the Masai Mara. The changing vegetation and the active wildlife make for exciting and unpredictable safari experiences.

- **Birdwatching:** March is a delightful time for birdwatching enthusiasts. The combination of resident bird species and the arrival of migratory birds creates a vibrant avian haven. Spot colorful species, including raptors, waterbirds, and numerous smaller birds.

- **Cultural Interactions:** Engage with the Maasai community and learn about their customs, traditions, and way of life. Visit Maasai villages, witness traditional dances, and gain insights into their unique relationship with wildlife.

- **Photography:** The dramatic weather patterns, vibrant landscapes, and wildlife interactions during the rainy season offer excellent opportunities for photography. Capture the lush greenery, animals in action, and the breathtaking beauty of the Masai Mara.

Tips:

- Pack both lightweight and rainproof clothing to be prepared for varying weather conditions. Layering options are essential to adjust to temperature fluctuations.

- Carry waterproof protection for your camera equipment to safeguard against unexpected showers.

- Embrace the unpredictable nature of the weather and be flexible with your safari activities to make the most of wildlife sightings and photographic opportunities.

In March, the Masai Mara unveils its transitional charm, showcasing the resilience of wildlife amid changing seasons. With its blend of natural wonders, diverse wildlife, and cultural immersion, this month promises a unique and enriching safari experience. Prepare to embrace the vibrant landscapes, witness captivating wildlife encounters, and connect with the rich cultural heritage of the Masai Mara.

April

April is part of the long rainy season in the Masai Mara, and while the weather can be unpredictable, it creates a vibrant and dynamic atmosphere. The landscape is adorned with lush vegetation, providing a stunning backdrop for wildlife encounters. It is a time of rejuvenation, as the rains nourish the land and trigger an abundance of life. Exploring the Masai Mara in April offers a unique opportunity to witness the raw beauty of nature and the resilience of the wildlife that thrives in this remarkable ecosystem.

i. **Weather:** April experiences occasional showers and increased rainfall compared to previous months. The temperatures remain warm, with daytime averages ranging from 25°C to 30°C (77°F to 86°F), while nighttime temperatures range from 15°C to 20°C (59°F to 68°F). It's essential to be prepared for the possibility of rain showers and wet conditions during your visit.

ii. Wildlife Highlights: While the rainy season can make wildlife sightings more challenging, April presents its own set of highlights and unique encounters. The abundance of vegetation attracts herbivores, and their presence, in turn, draws predators. Witnessing predator-prey interactions amidst the green landscapes can be a thrilling experience. Additionally, April is an excellent time for birdwatching, as migratory bird species join the resident bird population, adding to the diversity of avian species in the region.

Activities:

- **Game Drives:** Embark on game drives to explore the vast plains of the Masai Mara, keeping a keen eye out for wildlife sightings. The lush vegetation offers a picturesque backdrop, and with the presence of herbivores and predators, you can witness captivating wildlife interactions.

- **Birdwatching:** April is a fantastic time for birdwatching enthusiasts, as migratory bird species join the resident bird population. The diverse birdlife includes raptors, waterbirds, and a variety of smaller birds, providing ample opportunities for observation and photography.

- **Cultural Interactions:** Engage with the Maasai community to learn about their traditions, customs, and way of life. Visit Maasai villages, witness traditional dances, and gain insights into their harmonious relationship with the environment.

- **Photography:** The lush green landscapes, dramatic skies, and unique wildlife encounters in April offer excellent opportunities for photography. Capture the vibrant colors, dramatic lighting, and intimate moments of the wildlife in their natural habitat.

Tips:

- Pack lightweight, breathable clothing suitable for warm temperatures during the day. Be prepared for rain showers by including a rain jacket or poncho in your gear.
- Protect your camera equipment with waterproof covers or a dry bag to ensure it remains safe from the occasional rain showers.
- Embrace the beauty of the changing weather and the vibrant landscapes, as they offer a unique perspective on the Masai Mara.

In April, the Masai Mara reveals a different side of its natural splendor, showcasing the resilience of wildlife and the captivating beauty of a verdant landscape. With its rich biodiversity, lush vegetation, and cultural experiences, this month presents a distinctive safari adventure. Prepare to witness the wonders of nature, capture memorable photographs, and immerse yourself in the dynamic environment of the Masai Mara in April.

May

May offers a tranquil and serene experience in the Masai Mara as it falls towards the end of the long rainy season. The landscapes are adorned with lush vegetation, creating a picturesque backdrop for wildlife encounters. With fewer crowds and a sense of exclusivity, May provides an opportunity to immerse yourself in the tranquility of nature and witness the resilience of the wildlife that thrives in this remarkable ecosystem.

i.   **Weather:** In May, the Masai Mara experiences the tail end of the long rainy season. While rainfall decreases compared to earlier months, occasional showers are still possible. The temperatures remain warm, with average daytime temperatures ranging from 25°C to 30°C (77°F to 86°F). Nights can be cooler, with temperatures ranging from 15°C to 20°C (59°F to 68°F). It's advisable to pack both light and rainproof clothing to accommodate varying weather conditions.

ii. **Wildlife Highlights:** May presents an opportunity to witness the abundant wildlife in the Masai Mara. The lush vegetation attracts herbivores, creating a picturesque scene. The predator-prey dynamics continue, and predators such as lions, leopards, and cheetahs take advantage of the thriving prey populations. Additionally, May is an excellent time for birdwatching, with resident and migratory bird species providing a vibrant display of avian life.

Activities:

- **Game Drives:** May offers excellent game drive opportunities with the chance to spot a wide range of wildlife. Traverse the verdant landscapes and encounter herds of wildebeest, zebras, elephants, giraffes, and other iconic African wildlife. The predator sightings are also notable during this time.

- **Birdwatching:** Explore the diverse birdlife of the Masai Mara in May. Spot colorful migratory birds, raptors, waterbirds, and numerous smaller bird species. The lush vegetation provides a rich habitat for a variety of avian life.

- **Nature Walks:** Take guided nature walks to explore the smaller aspects of the ecosystem. Learn about the different plant species, insect life, and tracks left by wildlife. It's an opportunity to connect with nature on a more intimate level.

- **Cultural Interactions:** Engage with the Maasai community and learn about their rich cultural heritage. Visit Maasai villages, participate in traditional dances, and gain insights into their customs, traditions, and coexistence with wildlife.

Tips:

- Pack a mix of lightweight, breathable clothing and a rain jacket or poncho to be prepared for occasional showers.
- Mosquito repellent and sunscreen are essential items to include in your packing list.
- Embrace the tranquility and serenity of the Masai Mara in May. Take your time to soak

in the beauty of the landscape and the wildlife encounters.

In May, the Masai Mara unveils its serene and secluded side, offering a unique safari experience away from the peak tourist season. With its lush green landscapes, abundant wildlife, and cultural immersion opportunities, this month provides a chance to connect with nature and appreciate the delicate balance of life in the Masai Mara. Prepare to embark on an unforgettable journey filled with tranquility, wildlife encounters, and the natural wonders of this remarkable destination.

June

June in the Masai Mara signals the beginning of the dry season, characterized by cooler temperatures and clear skies. The landscape transforms as the grasses start to wither, revealing vast plains and making wildlife easier to spot. It is a time of anticipation, as the wildlife congregates around remaining water sources, leading to incredible predator-prey interactions. June offers a remarkable safari experience for nature enthusiasts, photographers, and those seeking a deeper connection with the wilderness.

i. **Weather:** In June, the Masai Mara experiences pleasant weather with cooler temperatures. Daytime temperatures range from 22°C to 28°C (72°F to 82°F), providing comfortable conditions for outdoor activities. Nights can be cooler, with temperatures ranging from 10°C to 15°C (50°F to 59°F), so it's advisable to pack some warm clothing for early morning and evening game drives.

ii. **Wildlife Highlights:** June brings an abundance of wildlife to the Masai Mara as water sources become scarce. The wildlife congregates around remaining waterholes and rivers, creating incredible opportunities for predator-prey interactions. Lions, leopards, cheetahs, and other predators are more active during this time, making it a thrilling period for wildlife sightings. Additionally, June is a great time to spot elephants, giraffes, zebras, and a variety of antelope species.

Activities:

- **Game Drives:** Explore the Masai Mara's vast plains on game drives, taking advantage of the favorable weather and increased wildlife visibility. Experienced guides will navigate you through the park, increasing your chances of encountering the iconic wildlife that roams the savannah.

- **Birdwatching:** June offers excellent birdwatching opportunities as resident and migratory bird species continue to thrive. Spot a variety of raptors, waterbirds, and smaller bird species, adding to the diverse avian population of the Masai Mara.

- **Hot Air Balloon Safaris:** Experience the breathtaking beauty of the Masai Mara from a unique perspective by taking a hot air balloon safari. Drift above the savannah at sunrise, witnessing the wildlife from a bird's-eye view and capturing incredible photographs.

- **Cultural Interactions:** Engage with the Maasai community to gain insights into their traditional way of life. Visit Maasai villages, interact with the locals, and learn about their customs, ceremonies, and conservation efforts.

Tips:

- Layer your clothing to accommodate temperature fluctuations throughout the day. Don't forget to include warmer clothing for the cooler mornings and evenings.

- Sun protection, including sunscreen, a hat, and sunglasses, is essential, as the African sun can still be strong even in the dry season.
- Consider booking your accommodations and safaris in advance, as June is a popular time to visit the Masai Mara.

In June, the Masai Mara invites you to witness the breathtaking drama of predator-prey interactions and the remarkable resilience of wildlife in the face of changing seasons. With its cooler temperatures, incredible wildlife sightings, and opportunities for cultural immersion, June provides a rewarding safari experience in this captivating destination. Prepare to embark on an unforgettable journey into the heart of the Masai Mara, where nature's wonders and wildlife encounters await.

July

July is synonymous with the Great Migration, a massive movement of wildebeest, zebras, and other herbivores as they traverse the vast plains of the Masai Mara. It is a time of incredible drama and intensity as millions of animals make their way across the Mara River, facing formidable challenges and providing an extraordinary wildlife spectacle. July also offers favorable weather conditions, making it an ideal time for safari enthusiasts and photographers to capture iconic moments in the Masai Mara.

i. **Weather:** In July, the Masai Mara experiences cool and dry weather, creating comfortable conditions for outdoor activities. Daytime temperatures range from 20°C to 25°C (68°F to 77°F), while nighttime temperatures can drop to around 10°C to 15°C (50°F to 59°F). The skies are generally clear, and rainfall is minimal, allowing for uninterrupted wildlife viewing and exceptional photographic opportunities.

ii. **Wildlife Highlights - The Great Migration:** The Great Migration is the centerpiece of July in the Masai Mara. Millions of wildebeest, accompanied by zebras and other herbivores, undertake a treacherous journey across the Mara River in search of fresh grazing lands. This dramatic river crossing attracts crocodiles, lions, and other predators, creating thrilling scenes of survival, struggle, and triumph. Witnessing this spectacle is an awe-inspiring experience that showcases the raw power and resilience of nature.

Activities:

- **Great Migration Game Drives:** Embark on game drives to witness the Great Migration up close. Follow the herds as they traverse the plains, witness river crossings, and observe the predator-prey interactions that unfold during this monumental event. Experienced guides and drivers will ensure you have the best vantage points to witness this natural phenomenon.

- **Hot Air Balloon Safaris:** Experience the grandeur of the Great Migration from a unique perspective by taking a hot air balloon safari. Float above the savannah at sunrise, capturing breathtaking aerial views of the vast herds and the stunning landscape below.

- **Wildlife Photography:** July provides exceptional opportunities for wildlife photography. Capture the raw emotions, stunning landscapes, and intimate moments of the Great Migration. The golden light, dynamic compositions, and dramatic river crossings present endless possibilities for memorable photographs.

- **Cultural Interactions:** Engage with the Maasai community and learn about their rich cultural heritage. Immerse yourself in their traditions, visit Maasai villages, and participate in cultural activities, offering a deeper understanding of the local way of life.

Tips:

- Book accommodations and safaris well in advance, as July is a peak tourist season due to the Great Migration.
- Pack warm clothing for the cooler mornings and evenings, including a jacket or sweater, as temperatures can be chilly during early game drives.
- Bring a telephoto lens and a sturdy tripod for capturing detailed wildlife and action shots during the Great Migration.

In July, the Masai Mara showcases one of the most awe-inspiring natural events on Earth - the Great Migration. Witnessing this extraordinary spectacle is an unforgettable experience that combines the raw power of nature with the delicate balance of survival. With favorable weather conditions, incredible wildlife sightings, and the cultural richness of the Maasai community, July promises a journey of a lifetime in the Masai Mara. Prepare to be captivated by the majesty and drama of the Great Migration, as the Masai Mara welcomes you to witness the wonders of nature in all their glory.

August

August in the Masai Mara is synonymous with the Great Migration, a breathtaking spectacle that unfolds as millions of wildebeest, zebras, and other herbivores navigate the vast plains in search of fresh grazing lands. It is a time of immense drama and survival, showcasing the raw power and resilience of nature. August also offers pleasant weather, clear skies, and incredible wildlife viewing opportunities, making it a prime month for those seeking an immersive safari experience.

i. **Weather:** During August, the Masai Mara experiences dry and mild weather, providing comfortable conditions for exploration. Daytime temperatures range from 20°C to 25°C (68°F to 77°F), while nighttime temperatures can drop to around 10°C to 15°C (50°F to 59°F). The skies are generally clear, and rainfall is minimal, allowing for uninterrupted wildlife encounters and enjoyable outdoor activities.

ii. **Wildlife Highlights - The Great Migration:** August marks a pivotal stage in the Great Migration, as the herds continue their journey across the Masai Mara. Witnessing the river crossings becomes even more thrilling as the animals face the perilous Mara River, teeming with crocodiles and other predators. The high concentration of herbivores attracts predators such as lions, leopards, cheetahs, and hyenas, resulting in spectacular wildlife interactions. The Great Migration is a once-in-a-lifetime experience that showcases the awe-inspiring resilience and instincts of these magnificent creatures.

Activities:

- **Great Migration Game Drives:** Embark on game drives to witness the Great Migration unfold before your eyes. Follow the herds as they traverse the plains, capturing the breathtaking river crossings and observing the predator-prey dynamics that accompany this extraordinary event. Knowledgeable guides will provide insights and ensure you have the best opportunities for wildlife sightings.

- **Hot Air Balloon Safaris:** Take to the skies on a hot air balloon safari, offering a unique perspective of the Great Migration. Drift above the vast savannahs, watching the herds move below and capturing stunning aerial views of the landscape. This enchanting experience provides a bird's-eye view of the natural wonders of the Masai Mara.

- **Wildlife Photography:** August presents excellent opportunities for wildlife photography. Capture the intense emotions, captivating interactions, and stunning landscapes of the Great Migration. The golden light, dramatic river crossings, and abundant wildlife create ideal conditions for capturing remarkable images.

- **Cultural Immersion:** Engage with the Maasai community and delve into their rich cultural heritage. Visit Maasai villages, participate in traditional ceremonies, and learn about their way of life and the importance of coexistence with wildlife.

Tips:

- Plan your trip well in advance, as August is a popular time to visit the Masai Mara due to the Great Migration.
- Pack layers of clothing to accommodate temperature changes throughout the day. Don't forget to bring warm clothing for early morning and evening game drives.
- Carry essential camera gear, including a telephoto lens, extra memory cards, and spare batteries for capturing the incredible wildlife moments.

In August, the Masai Mara showcases the pinnacle of the Great Migration, offering a front-row seat to one of nature's most extraordinary events. With its captivating wildlife encounters, pleasant weather, and cultural experiences, this month presents a unique opportunity to witness the power and resilience of the animal kingdom. Prepare to be immersed in the wonders of the Masai Mara as you witness the breathtaking scenes of the Great Migration and create lifelong memories in this incredible African wilderness.

September

September is a transitional month in the Masai Mara, offering a mix of dry and rainy season characteristics. It is a time of anticipation as the landscape begins to transform with the arrival of short rains. September offers travelers a unique opportunity to witness the final chapters of the Great Migration, along with pleasant weather and abundant wildlife sightings. Whether you are a nature enthusiast, a wildlife photographer, or a cultural explorer, September promises an immersive experience in the Masai Mara.

i. **Weather:** In September, the Masai Mara experiences a transition from the dry season to the short rainy season. The temperatures are still relatively warm, with daytime averages ranging from 22°C to 28°C (72°F to 82°F). However, the nights and early mornings can be cooler, with temperatures ranging from 10°C to 15°C (50°F to 59°F). It's important to note that September is characterized by the possibility of rainfall, so be prepared for occasional showers and pack appropriate rain gear.

ii. **Wildlife Highlights:** September offers a wealth of wildlife sightings in the Masai Mara. The Great Migration continues, with wildebeest, zebras, and other herbivores making their way back towards the Serengeti in Tanzania. Witnessing the herds crossing the Mara River, navigating through grasslands, and encountering predators is a remarkable experience. In addition, September provides excellent opportunities to spot resident wildlife, including lions, elephants, giraffes, and various antelope species.

Activities:

- **Great Migration Game Drives:** Embark on game drives to witness the final stages of the Great Migration. Follow the herds as they navigate the plains and make their way back to the Serengeti. Witness the intense river crossings, predator-prey interactions, and the resilience of the wildlife during this pivotal time.

- **Wildlife Photography:** September presents incredible photography opportunities. Capture the dramatic moments of the Great Migration, the lush green landscapes, and the unique animal behavior that unfolds during this transitional period. Be prepared to adapt your photography techniques to changing light conditions.

- **Birdwatching:** September is an excellent time for birdwatching in the Masai Mara. Resident and migratory bird species can be spotted, making it a paradise for bird enthusiasts. Keep an eye out for raptors, waterbirds, and smaller bird species displaying vibrant plumage.

- **Cultural Experiences:** Engage with the Maasai community to learn about their traditions, customs, and sustainable practices. Visit Maasai villages, witness traditional ceremonies, and gain insights into their harmonious coexistence with wildlife.

Tips:

- Pack both lightweight and rainproof clothing to be prepared for varying weather conditions. Include a rain jacket or poncho, as September can experience occasional showers.
- Carry insect repellent and sunscreen to protect yourself from insects and the sun during outdoor activities.
- Embrace the changing landscape and the possibility of rainfall, as it adds a unique touch to your safari experience.

In September, the Masai Mara presents a transition between seasons, with the Great Migration reaching its climax and the arrival of the short rainy season. It is a time of change, providing travelers with a rich tapestry of wildlife encounters, cultural immersion, and the beauty of nature's transformation. Prepare to witness the grand finale of the Great Migration, capture incredible photographs, and embrace the allure of the Masai Mara in September.

October

October in the Masai Mara signifies the arrival of the short dry season, characterized by warm days, cooler nights, and the gradual retreat of the long rains. It is a period of changing landscapes, as the grasses begin to wither, making wildlife more visible. October offers a serene and intimate experience, with fewer crowds and ample opportunities to witness remarkable wildlife encounters. Whether you're an avid wildlife enthusiast, a birdwatching enthusiast, or seeking cultural immersion, October provides an enriching journey into the heart of the Masai Mara.

i.   **Weather:** During October, the Masai Mara experiences pleasant weather, with temperatures gradually increasing. Daytime temperatures range from 25°C to 30°C (77°F to 86°F), providing comfortable conditions for outdoor activities. Nights can be cooler, with temperatures ranging from 15°C to 20°C (59°F to 68°F). The skies are generally clear, offering excellent visibility and beautiful sunsets, creating a picturesque backdrop for your adventures.

ii. **Wildlife Highlights:** October offers abundant wildlife sightings in the Masai Mara as the vegetation starts to thin out. The wildlife congregates around remaining water sources, providing excellent opportunities for predator-prey interactions. Lions, cheetahs, leopards, and other predators become more active, making it an exciting time for wildlife encounters. Additionally, October presents fantastic birdwatching opportunities, with resident and migratory bird species showcasing their vibrant plumage.

Activities:

- **Game Drives:** Explore the Masai Mara's vast savannahs on game drives, venturing into different areas to encounter a variety of wildlife species. As the vegetation thins out, it becomes easier to spot animals, including elephants, giraffes, zebras, and various antelope species. Experienced guides will enhance your safari experience with their knowledge and expertise.

- **Birdwatching:** October is a wonderful time for birdwatching enthusiasts. Spot a diverse range of bird species, including raptors, waterbirds, and smaller colorful birds. The open landscapes and clearer visibility allow for excellent bird sightings and photography opportunities.

- **Cultural Immersion:** Engage with the Maasai community to learn about their traditions, culture, and sustainable practices. Visit Maasai villages, interact with the locals, and experience traditional dances and ceremonies. Gain insights into their deep connection with the land and wildlife.

- **Photography:** October presents incredible photography opportunities in the Masai Mara. Capture stunning images of wildlife against the backdrop of golden grasslands and expansive skies. The clarity of the landscape and the dramatic lighting conditions provide a perfect canvas for your photography skills.

Tips:

- Pack lightweight and breathable clothing suitable for warm temperatures during the day. Bring a sweater or jacket for cooler mornings and evenings.

- Protect yourself from the sun by wearing a hat, sunglasses, and applying sunscreen.
- Be prepared for potential changes in weather patterns, including the possibility of occasional showers.

In October, the Masai Mara reveals its tranquil and captivating side, offering a serene safari experience amidst remarkable wildlife encounters. With pleasant weather, abundant wildlife sightings, and cultural immersion opportunities, this month provides a fantastic opportunity to connect with the beauty of nature and the rich heritage of the Masai Mara. Prepare to embark on an unforgettable journey, capturing the essence of the changing landscape and creating lasting memories in this extraordinary African wilderness.

November

November is a period of transition in the Masai Mara, as the long rainy season gradually takes hold. It is a time of anticipation and transformation, as the landscape starts to rejuvenate with fresh greenery, new growth, and the return of migratory bird species. November offers a more tranquil and secluded experience, with fewer visitors, abundant wildlife, and the chance to witness the natural cycles of the Masai Mara. Whether you seek wildlife adventures, birdwatching opportunities, or cultural immersion, November provides a unique safari experience.

i. **Weather:** In November, the Masai Mara experiences increasing rainfall as the long rainy season begins. Daytime temperatures range from 22°C to 28°C (72°F to 82°F), providing comfortable conditions for outdoor activities. Nights can be cooler, with temperatures ranging from 15°C to 20°C (59°F to 68°F). It's essential to be prepared for rain showers and pack appropriate rain gear, including a waterproof jacket or poncho.

ii. **Wildlife Highlights:** November brings diverse wildlife sightings in the Masai Mara as the landscape transforms with the onset of rains. The rejuvenated vegetation attracts herbivores, resulting in an abundance of wildlife. You can witness newborn animals, including wildebeest calves and zebra foals, as well as an increase in predator activity. Lions, cheetahs, leopards, and other predators take advantage of the plentiful prey, offering thrilling wildlife encounters.

Activities:

▪ **Game Drives:** Embark on game drives to explore the Masai Mara's picturesque landscapes and encounter a wide range of wildlife species. The lush greenery provides a stunning backdrop for wildlife photography, and the increased predator-prey interactions make for exciting sightings.

- **Birdwatching:** November is a fantastic time for birdwatching enthusiasts as migratory bird species return to the Masai Mara. Spot a plethora of colorful birds, including raptors, waterbirds, and smaller bird species. The varied habitats and the fresh growth of vegetation make for a rich avian spectacle.

- **Cultural Interactions:** Engage with the Maasai community and immerse yourself in their vibrant culture. Visit Maasai villages, learn about their traditional way of life, participate in cultural activities, and gain insights into their deep connection with the land and wildlife.

- **Nature Walks:** Take guided nature walks to explore the smaller aspects of the Masai Mara ecosystem. Observe the intricate details of plants, insects, and tracks left by wildlife, and learn about the fascinating ecological processes taking place.

Tips:

- Pack lightweight, breathable clothing suitable for warm temperatures during the day. Include a waterproof jacket or poncho to stay dry during rain showers.
- Carry insect repellent and sunscreen to protect yourself from insects and the sun.
- Embrace the changing weather patterns and the lush green landscapes as they add a unique touch to your safari experience.

In November, the Masai Mara reveals its transformational beauty, with fresh growth, newborn wildlife, and a sense of renewal. With its diverse wildlife encounters, vibrant birdlife, and cultural immersion opportunities, this month provides an enriching safari experience. Prepare to embrace the changing landscapes, witness the remarkable wildlife interactions, and connect with the spirit of the Masai Mara in November.

December

December in the Masai Mara is a time of transformation and natural rejuvenation as the short rainy season reaches its peak. The landscape flourishes with fresh greenery, vibrant flowers, and flowing rivers, creating a picturesque backdrop for unforgettable wildlife encounters. It is a time of abundance, with newborn animals, plentiful birdlife, and an array of wildlife species thriving in the revitalized ecosystem. Whether you seek wildlife adventures, birdwatching opportunities, or cultural immersion, December offers a captivating safari experience.

i. **Weather:** In December, the Masai Mara experiences the height of the short rainy season, resulting in increased rainfall and occasional thunderstorms. Daytime temperatures range from 22°C to 28°C (72°F to 82°F), providing comfortable conditions for outdoor activities. Nights can be cooler, with temperatures ranging from 15°C to 20°C (59°F to 68°F). It's essential to pack lightweight, waterproof clothing, including a rain jacket or poncho, to stay dry during rain showers.

ii. **Wildlife Highlights:** December brings abundant wildlife sightings in the Masai Mara as the landscape thrives with fresh vegetation. The newborn animals, including wildebeest calves, zebra foals, and other herbivores, are a delightful sight. Predators are also active during this time, taking advantage of the plentiful prey. Lions, cheetahs, leopards, and other carnivores provide thrilling wildlife encounters, creating a dynamic and dramatic safari experience.

Activities:

- **Game Drives:** Embark on game drives to explore the Masai Mara's lush landscapes and encounter a diverse array of wildlife species. The vibrant greenery provides a stunning backdrop for wildlife photography, and the increased predator-prey interactions make for exciting sightings.

- **Birdwatching:** December is an excellent time for birdwatching in the Masai Mara, as migratory bird species join the resident bird population. Spot a multitude of colorful birds, including raptors, waterbirds, and smaller bird species. The flourishing vegetation and the presence of water bodies create a haven for birdlife.

- **Cultural Immersion:** Engage with the Maasai community and immerse yourself in their rich cultural heritage. Visit Maasai villages, learn about their traditional practices and rituals, participate in cultural activities, and gain insights into their deep connection with the land and wildlife.

- **Nature Walks:** Take guided nature walks to explore the intricate details of the Masai Mara's ecosystem. Observe the diverse plant life, insects, and tracks left by wildlife, and learn about the ecological processes that take place during the rainy season.

Tips:

- Pack lightweight, breathable clothing suitable for warm temperatures during the day. Include a rain jacket or poncho to stay dry during rain showers.

- Carry insect repellent and sunscreen to protect yourself from insects and the sun.
- Embrace the vibrant landscapes, the fresh growth of vegetation, and the occasional rain showers, as they add a unique touch to your safari experience.

In December, the Masai Mara unveils its revitalized and flourishing beauty, offering a captivating safari experience amidst remarkable wildlife encounters. With its lush landscapes, vibrant birdlife, and cultural immersion opportunities, this month provides a rewarding journey into the heart of nature. Prepare to witness the marvels of newborn animals, capture breathtaking photographs, and embrace the spirit of the Masai Mara in December.

By considering the monthly breakdown and activities offered in each period, you can choose the best time to visit the Masai Mara that aligns with your interests and expectations, ensuring a memorable and rewarding experience in this extraordinary wildlife haven.

4 weeks itinerary in Masai Mara perfect for first timers

Embarking on a four-week itinerary in the Masai Mara is an ideal way for first-time visitors to immerse themselves in the beauty, wildlife, and cultural heritage of this iconic safari destination. With ample time to explore the diverse landscapes and encounter the abundant wildlife, this itinerary allows for a comprehensive experience that captures the essence of the Masai Mara. From thrilling game drives to cultural interactions, this four-week journey promises an unforgettable adventure. In this guide, we will provide an introduction and details on a perfect four-week itinerary in the Masai Mara for first-time visitors.

Week 1: Getting Acquainted with the Masai Mara

During the first week of your four-week itinerary in the Masai Mara, you will have the opportunity to get acquainted with the vastness and beauty of this iconic safari destination. This week focuses on exploration, orientation, and experiencing the diverse wildlife that inhabits the region.

Days 1-2: Arrival and Orientation

Upon arrival in the Masai Mara, take some time to settle into your accommodations and get acclimated to the surroundings. Take a moment to appreciate the natural beauty of the landscape, the sounds of the wilderness, and the warmth of the African hospitality. Meet with your guide or tour operator to discuss the itinerary, clarify any questions, and align your expectations for the upcoming days.

Days 3-6: Game Drives and Wildlife Encounters

Embark on daily game drives to explore different areas of the Masai Mara. Accompanied by experienced guides, venture deep into the wilderness and witness the incredible biodiversity that the reserve has to offer. The Masai Mara is home to an abundance of wildlife, including the renowned Big Five - lions, elephants, buffalos, leopards, and rhinoceros. Observe their natural behaviors, track their movements, and learn about their conservation status from your knowledgeable guides.

Game drives during this week will allow you to explore the diverse landscapes of the Masai Mara, from open grasslands to acacia-dotted savannahs and winding riverbanks. Your guides will navigate through the terrain, seeking out the best vantage points and ensuring optimal wildlife sightings. Keep your camera ready to capture breathtaking moments and create memories that will last a lifetime.

Take time to appreciate the smaller creatures too, such as cheetahs, hyenas, giraffes, zebras, and various antelope species that roam the plains. Listen to the symphony of birdcalls as you scan the skies for eagles, vultures, and other avian species. Engage in conversation with your guides, who will share their extensive knowledge about the flora, fauna, and cultural significance of the Masai Mara.

In the evenings, relax at your accommodations and reflect on the day's adventures. Swap stories with fellow travelers and indulge in delicious meals that showcase local flavors. Take advantage of any optional activities offered by your lodge, such as guided nature walks or cultural performances, to further enrich your experience.

During Week 1, you will lay the foundation for an unforgettable safari experience by acquainting yourself with the beauty and wildlife of the Masai Mara. Stay tuned for Week 2 as you delve deeper into the captivating wonders of this remarkable African wilderness.

Week 2: Great Migration and Cultural Immersion

During the second week of your four-week itinerary in the Masai Mara, you will have the incredible opportunity to witness the awe-inspiring Great Migration and immerse yourself in the vibrant culture of the Maasai community. This week combines thrilling wildlife encounters with unique cultural experiences, providing a well-rounded and unforgettable safari adventure.

Days 7-11: Great Migration Experience

Embark on a journey to witness the world-famous Great Migration. During these days, you will have the opportunity to witness the dramatic river crossings as millions of wildebeest, zebras, and other herbivores traverse the treacherous Mara River, braving the jaws of crocodiles and the pursuit of predators. Your experienced guides will position you at strategic points along the riverbanks to witness this remarkable spectacle up close. Prepare to be captivated by the sight of herds thundering across the plains, creating a dramatic scene of survival and perseverance.

Take time to observe the dynamics between predator and prey as lions, cheetahs, leopards, and hyenas capitalize on the abundance of prey. Your guides will provide valuable insights into the behavior and strategies of these remarkable animals, enhancing your understanding and appreciation of the ecosystem.

Days 12-14: Cultural Interactions

Immerse yourself in the vibrant culture of the Maasai community, one of the most iconic indigenous groups in East Africa. Engage in cultural interactions and gain a deeper understanding of their traditions, customs, and way of life. Visit Maasai villages and be welcomed by the warm hospitality of the locals. Participate in traditional dances, learn about their livestock-keeping practices, and witness unique ceremonies. Spend time with Maasai elders and community leaders who will share stories and legends, providing insight into the deep connection between the Maasai people and the land. Gain an appreciation for their sustainable practices and their harmonious coexistence with wildlife. You may have the opportunity to engage in community projects or support local initiatives, contributing to the well-being of the community.

Throughout this week, you will have the chance to capture incredible photographs that showcase both the wildlife and the vibrant Maasai culture. Engage in meaningful conversations with your guides and fellow travelers, fostering cultural understanding and creating lasting memories.

During Week 2, you will witness the magnificence of the Great Migration and immerse yourself in the vibrant Maasai culture, creating unforgettable memories and deepening your connection to the Masai Mara. Stay tuned for Week 3 as you continue your journey through this captivating safari destination.

Week 3: Photographic Safari and Birdwatching

During the third week of your four-week itinerary in the Masai Mara, you will focus on honing your photography skills and exploring the diverse birdlife of the region. This week is dedicated to capturing stunning images of wildlife and immersing yourself in the fascinating world of avian species.

Days 15-21: Photography-focused Safari

Embark on specialized game drives and guided walks that cater to photography enthusiasts. Your experienced guides will take you to prime locations, positioning you for the best opportunities to capture remarkable wildlife moments. Utilize the golden light of the early morning and late afternoon to enhance the beauty of your photographs. Take the time to observe animal behavior and anticipate their movements, allowing you to capture dynamic shots. Experiment with different techniques, such as panning to capture motion, playing with depth of field to create stunning bokeh, and utilizing natural framing to add visual interest to your images.

Your guides will share their expertise, offering tips on composition, lighting, and camera settings. They will also help you identify potential subjects and provide insights into the behavior and biology of the wildlife you encounter. Embrace the opportunity to learn and grow as a photographer in this incredible setting.

Days 22-24: Birdwatching Haven

Dedicate this part of the week to exploring the rich birdlife of the Masai Mara. Join guided birdwatching walks and drives led by experienced ornithologists who will help you identify various bird species and their distinct calls. The Masai Mara is home to an incredible diversity of birdlife, including raptors, waterbirds, and smaller colorful birds. Keep your binoculars and camera ready as you explore different habitats, including riverbanks, wetlands, and acacia woodlands. Look out for magnificent raptors such as eagles, falcons, and hawks soaring through the skies. Observe the fascinating behavior of waterbirds, including herons, storks, and kingfishers, as they navigate the rivers and wetlands. Take delight in spotting smaller birds, from colorful bee-eaters to cheerful sunbirds, and marvel at their intricate plumage.

Your birdwatching guides will share their knowledge about the birds' habitat, migratory patterns, and conservation status. They will help you create a checklist of the species you encounter, allowing you to track your birdwatching progress and cherish the memories of these avian encounters.

During Week 3, you will have the opportunity to refine your photography skills and explore the diverse birdlife of the Masai Mara. Through dedicated game drives and birdwatching activities, you will capture stunning images and expand your knowledge of avian species. Stay tuned for Week 4 as you continue your journey through this remarkable safari destination.

Week 4: Conservation and Cultural Experiences

During the fourth and final week of your four-week itinerary in the Masai Mara, you will have the opportunity to engage in conservation initiatives and deepen your cultural understanding. This week focuses on giving back to the community and actively participating in efforts to preserve the natural environment and support local communities.

Days 25-28: Conservation and Community Engagement

Immerse yourself in the conservation initiatives of the Masai Mara. Participate in activities that contribute to the preservation of this remarkable ecosystem. Join local conservation organizations and rangers on guided walks or drives to learn about their efforts in wildlife monitoring, anti-poaching measures, and habitat restoration. Gain insights into the challenges and successes of conservation in the Masai Mara. You may have the opportunity to get involved in tree planting projects or assist in wildlife monitoring programs. These hands-on experiences will allow you to actively contribute to the long-term sustainability of the Masai Mara's natural resources.

Additionally, engage with local communities to understand their way of life and support their livelihoods. Visit local schools and healthcare facilities to learn about the challenges they face and the impact of community-driven initiatives. Connect with artisans and craftsmen to appreciate their traditional skills and support their local businesses.

Spend time with Maasai elders, engaging in meaningful conversations about the Maasai people's rich cultural heritage. Learn about their traditional conservation practices and their deep connection with the land and wildlife. Participate in traditional ceremonies, such as storytelling sessions and dance performances, and gain a deeper appreciation for the importance of cultural preservation. Reflect on the experiences of the past weeks and share your journey with fellow travelers and locals. Take the opportunity to educate others about the importance of responsible tourism and the significance of conservation efforts in safeguarding the Masai Mara for future generations.

During Week 4, you will actively contribute to conservation efforts and engage with local communities, creating a deeper connection to the Masai Mara. By participating in these experiences, you will leave a positive impact on the environment and the lives of the people who call this region home. Embrace the opportunity to make a difference and leave a legacy of sustainable travel.

A four-week itinerary in the Masai Mara allows first-time visitors to truly delve into the richness of this extraordinary safari destination. With a combination of wildlife encounters, cultural interactions, and opportunities for photography and conservation engagement, this itinerary promises an enriching and transformative journey in the heart of the Masai Mara. Prepare to be captivated by the wild beauty and cultural heritage of this remarkable African wilderness.

How to stay safe in Masai Mara

When visiting the Masai Mara, ensuring your safety is paramount to have a memorable and worry-free experience. The Masai Mara is a wilderness teeming with wildlife, and while it offers incredible opportunities for exploration and adventure, it's essential to be mindful of potential risks and take precautions to stay safe. In this guide, we will provide an introduction to help you stay safe in the Masai Mara, offering valuable tips and advice to ensure a secure and enjoyable journey. Here are some essential tips to help you stay safe in the Masai Mara:

i. **Travel with a reputable tour operator:** Choose a tour operator or travel agency with a good reputation and experience in organizing safaris in the Masai Mara. They will have knowledgeable guides who are familiar with the region and can ensure your safety throughout your trip.

ii. **Follow the guidance of your guide:** Listen to and follow the instructions provided by your guide or driver. They are experienced professionals who are well-versed in the local conditions, wildlife behavior, and potential risks. Always stay inside the vehicle unless instructed otherwise, and do not approach or attempt to touch any animals.

iii. **Respect wildlife and maintain a safe distance:** The Masai Mara is home to a wide range of wildlife, including predators. It is crucial to maintain a safe distance from animals and avoid any behavior that may agitate or provoke them. Respect their space and natural behavior, and never attempt to feed or touch the animals.

iv. **Be cautious during game drives and walking safaris:** Always remain seated and keep all body parts within the vehicle during game drives. If you participate in walking safaris or guided walks, follow your guide's instructions and stay together as a group. Do not wander off on your own and be attentive to your surroundings.

v. **Pack and use mosquito repellent:** The Masai Mara is located in a region where mosquitoes and other insects may be present. Protect yourself from mosquito-borne diseases by packing and using an effective mosquito repellent. Additionally, consider wearing long-sleeved clothing and pants during early mornings and evenings when mosquitoes are most active.

vi. **Stay hydrated and protect yourself from the sun:** Drink plenty of water to stay hydrated, especially during game drives when temperatures can be high. Protect yourself from the sun by wearing a hat, sunglasses, and sunscreen with a high SPF. Seek shade or use a sun umbrella if needed.

vii. **Be prepared for changes in weather:** The weather in the Masai Mara can be unpredictable, so it's essential to be prepared for potential changes. Pack layers of clothing that can be added or removed depending on the temperature. Carry a rain jacket or poncho in case of unexpected showers.

viii. **Secure your belongings:** Keep your personal belongings secure at all times, whether in your accommodations, vehicle, or public areas. Use lockable bags or safes when available and avoid displaying expensive items that may attract unwanted attention.

ix. **Respect local customs and traditions:** Familiarize yourself with the local customs and traditions of the Maasai community and the Kenyan culture in general. Show respect for their traditions, dress modestly when visiting communities, and seek permission before taking photographs.

x. **Stay updated on travel advisories:** Prior to your trip, check the latest travel advisories and safety recommendations for the Masai Mara and Kenya. Stay informed about any potential risks or concerns and adjust your plans accordingly.

By following these safety tips and being mindful of your surroundings, you can have a safe and enjoyable experience while exploring the beauty and wildlife of the Masai Mara. Remember that nature is unpredictable, and it is important to prioritize your safety and the well-being of the wildlife and local communities.

Best travel tips for saving money in Masai Mara

Traveling to the Masai Mara is a dream come true for many nature and wildlife enthusiasts. While it's a destination that offers incredible experiences and unforgettable encounters with wildlife, it's also essential to consider ways to save money during your visit. By implementing smart travel strategies and making informed choices, you can enjoy a budget-friendly trip without compromising on the quality of your experience. In this guide, we will provide an introduction and details on the best travel tips for saving money in the Masai Mara, allowing you to make the most of your journey while keeping your expenses in check.

i. **Plan your trip during the shoulder season:** Consider visiting the Masai Mara during the shoulder seasons, which fall between the peak and low seasons. During these periods, accommodation rates tend to be more affordable, and there are fewer crowds, allowing you to have a more exclusive experience.

ii. **Compare accommodation options:** Research and compare different accommodation options in and around the Masai Mara. Look for lodges, tented camps, or budget-friendly campsites that offer competitive rates without compromising on comfort and quality. Keep an eye out for special deals or discounted rates offered by accommodations.

iii. **Consider group or shared safaris:** Joining a group or shared safari can significantly reduce costs, as you'll be able to split the expenses with other travelers. Many tour operators and lodges offer shared safari packages, which allow you to enjoy game drives and wildlife encounters while sharing the costs with fellow travelers.

iv. **Opt for self-drive or budget-friendly transport options:** If you're comfortable driving in the region, consider renting a car and exploring the Masai Mara on a self-drive safari. This option gives you the flexibility to set your own schedule and can be more cost-effective than hiring a private driver or using guided tours. Alternatively, consider using public transportation or shared shuttle services to reach the Masai Mara.

v. **Pack snacks and water:** To save money on meals, pack snacks and bottled water for your game drives and excursions. This way, you can enjoy refreshments without relying solely on expensive lodge or camp meals. Be mindful of the environment and dispose of your waste responsibly.

vi. **Eat at local restaurants or markets:** Explore local eateries and markets in nearby towns or villages outside the Masai Mara reserve. These places often offer more affordable meal options and a chance to experience authentic Kenyan cuisine.

vii. **Book activities and tours directly:** When booking additional activities or tours, consider booking directly with local operators or guides instead of going through intermediaries or agents. This way, you can negotiate better rates and have more control over your expenses.

viii. **Be mindful of additional charges and fees:** When finalizing your booking, pay attention to any additional charges or fees that may be applicable, such as park entrance fees, conservation fees, or extra charges for certain activities. Understanding these costs in advance will help you budget accordingly.

ix. **Avoid unnecessary purchases and souvenirs:** Be mindful of impulse buying and think twice before making souvenir purchases. Consider supporting local artisans and businesses by purchasing directly from them instead of tourist shops that often have higher markups.

x. **Exchange currency in advance:** If possible, exchange currency before arriving in the Masai Mara or withdraw local currency from ATMs in major towns or cities. This way, you can avoid unfavorable exchange rates or additional fees charged at hotels or lodges.

By implementing these travel tips, you can save money without compromising your experience in the Masai Mara. With careful planning, budget-conscious choices, and a focus on value, you can embark on an affordable and fulfilling adventure in this stunning African wilderness.

Safety on the Trail

Safety is a paramount concern when venturing out on trails and hiking adventures. Whether you're exploring a scenic nature trail or embarking on a more challenging trek in the Masai Mara, prioritizing safety ensures an enjoyable and worry-free experience. Understanding potential risks, being prepared, and practicing caution are essential to mitigate any dangers that may arise. In this guide, we will provide an introduction and details on safety measures to consider when hiking and exploring trails in the Masai Mara, allowing you to make the most of your outdoor adventures while keeping yourself and others safe.

i.   **Research and choose appropriate trails:** Before setting out, research and choose trails that align with your fitness level, experience, and interests. Consider the duration, difficulty, and terrain of the trail, as well as any potential hazards or risks associated with it. This will help ensure you're adequately prepared for the journey ahead.

ii. **Check weather conditions:** Monitor the weather forecast before heading out on a trail. Avoid hiking during extreme weather conditions such as heavy rain, storms, or extreme heat, as these can pose safety risks. Be aware of seasonal variations and plan accordingly.

iii. **Inform others of your plans:** Always inform someone, such as a friend or family member, about your hiking plans, including the trail you're taking, estimated duration, and expected return time. This way, someone will be aware of your whereabouts and can take action if you encounter any difficulties or fail to return as scheduled.

iv. **Hike with a companion or in a group:** Whenever possible, hike with a companion or in a group. Having others with you enhances safety, as you can watch out for each other, provide assistance if needed, and share resources. If hiking alone, exercise additional caution and inform others about your solo adventure.

v. **Pack essential safety equipment:** Carry a well-equipped hiking backpack that includes essential safety items such as a first aid kit, extra food and water, a map and compass or GPS device, a headlamp or flashlight, a whistle, a multi-tool or pocket knife, and a fully charged mobile phone for emergencies. Consider additional items like a rain jacket, warm clothing, and sunscreen based on the weather conditions and trail requirements.

vi. **Dress appropriately and wear sturdy footwear:** Wear appropriate clothing for the trail, including moisture-wicking layers, comfortable hiking pants, and sturdy footwear that provides ankle support and good traction. Avoid wearing cotton clothing, as it retains moisture and can lead to discomfort and hypothermia in wet conditions.

vii.   **Stay on marked trails and follow signage:** Stick to marked trails and follow any signage or guidelines provided. Venturing off the trail can increase the risk of getting lost, encountering dangerous terrain, or disturbing fragile ecosystems. Respecting designated paths helps preserve the natural environment and minimizes potential harm to wildlife.

viii.   **Stay hydrated and nourished:** Carry an adequate supply of water and stay hydrated throughout your hike. Take regular breaks to rest and refuel with snacks or meals to maintain energy levels. Avoid drinking water from natural sources unless you have the means to purify it.

ix.   **Be cautious around wildlife:** The Masai Mara is home to diverse wildlife, and encountering animals on the trail is possible. Keep a safe distance, never approach or feed wildlife, and avoid surprising them. If you come across larger animals such as elephants or buffalo, give them a wide berth and observe from a safe distance.

x. **Trust your instincts and be prepared to turn back:** If you encounter unforeseen hazards, challenging weather conditions, or if you feel physically or mentally exhausted, trust your instincts and be prepared to turn back or alter your plans. Your safety should always be the top priority.

By following these safety guidelines, you can ensure a safer hiking experience in the Masai Mara. Remember to be prepared, stay vigilant, and make informed decisions along the trail. With caution and respect for nature, you can fully enjoy the breathtaking landscapes and incredible wilderness of the Masai Mara while minimizing potential risks.

Sunburn prevention strategies for your Masai Mara trip

The Masai Mara is a destination known for its stunning landscapes and abundant wildlife, offering travelers an opportunity to immerse themselves in the beauty of the African wilderness. However, it's crucial to protect your skin from the harsh sun rays during your Masai Mara trip. Sunburn can not only be painful but also pose long-term health risks. In this guide, we will provide an introduction and details on effective sunburn prevention strategies to ensure your skin stays protected and healthy throughout your Masai Mara adventure.

i. **Wear Sunscreen:** Apply a broad-spectrum sunscreen with a high SPF (Sun Protection Factor) of 30 or above. Choose a sunscreen that protects against both UVA and UVB rays. Apply it generously to all exposed areas of your body, including your face, neck, arms, and legs. Reapply every two hours, or more frequently if you've been sweating or swimming.

ii. **Seek Shade During Peak Hours:** The sun's rays are strongest between 10 a.m. and 4 p.m. Seek shade during these peak hours to minimize your exposure to direct sunlight. Plan your activities accordingly, such as scheduling indoor or shaded attractions, lunches, or relaxation time during this period.

iii. **Wear Protective Clothing:** Cover your skin with lightweight, loose-fitting, and light-colored clothing that provides adequate sun protection. Opt for long-sleeved shirts, long pants, and wide-brimmed hats to shield your face, neck, and ears from the sun. Consider wearing clothing made with UV-protective fabrics for added sun protection.

iv. **Wear Sunglasses:** Protect your eyes from harmful UV rays by wearing sunglasses that provide 100% UV protection. Look for sunglasses labeled with UV400 or 100% UV protection. Wrap-around styles offer additional protection by preventing sun rays from entering through the sides.

v. **Stay Hydrated:** Drink plenty of water to stay hydrated, as sun exposure can lead to dehydration. Carry a refillable water bottle and sip water frequently throughout the day, even if you don't feel thirsty. Staying hydrated helps maintain overall health and supports your skin's natural ability to protect itself.

vi. **Take Breaks in Shaded Areas:** If you're spending a significant amount of time outdoors, take regular breaks in shaded areas. This allows your skin to recover and reduces prolonged exposure to the sun. Look for shaded spots under trees, umbrellas, or built-in shelters during game drives or other outdoor activities.

vii. **Be Mindful of Reflection:** Remember that water, sand, snow, and other reflective surfaces can intensify the sun's rays and increase your risk of sunburn. Take extra precautions when you're near water bodies or areas with reflective surfaces, as you may be exposed to more UV radiation.

viii. **Use Lip Balm with SPF:** Protect your lips from sunburn by using a lip balm that contains SPF. Apply it frequently throughout the day, especially if you'll be exposed to the sun for an extended period.

ix. **Educate Yourself About Medications:** Certain medications, such as antibiotics or some acne treatments, can increase your skin's sensitivity to sunlight. If you're taking any medication, consult your healthcare provider or pharmacist to understand if it poses any sun-related risks. Take necessary precautions, such as applying extra sunscreen or avoiding excessive sun exposure if needed.

x. **Practice Healthy Sun Habits:** Make sun protection a habit in your daily routine, not just during your Masai Mara trip. Even on cloudy or overcast days, UV rays can still penetrate through the clouds and cause sunburn. Therefore, it's important to practice sun protection measures consistently, regardless of the weather.

By following these sunburn prevention strategies, you can enjoy your Masai Mara trip while safeguarding your skin from harmful sun damage. Remember, prevention is key, and taking proactive steps to protect your skin will contribute to your overall health and well-being during your African adventure.

Where to stay in Masai Mara

Choosing the right accommodation is crucial for a memorable and comfortable stay in the Masai Mara. Whether you prefer luxury lodges, intimate tented camps, or budget-friendly options, the Masai Mara offers a range of accommodations to suit every traveler's preferences and needs. In this guide, we will provide an introduction and details on different accommodation options available in the Masai Mara, helping you find the perfect place to stay and make the most of your safari experience.

i. **Luxury Lodges:** Luxury lodges in the Masai Mara offer unparalleled comfort, excellent service, and stunning views of the surrounding wilderness. These lodges often feature spacious suites or cottages with en-suite bathrooms, private verandas, and modern amenities. They may also offer additional facilities such as swimming pools, spa services, fine dining restaurants, and guided activities. Luxury lodges provide a high level of comfort and personalized service, ensuring a truly indulgent experience in the heart of the Masai Mara.

ii.   **Tented Camps:** Tented camps offer a unique and immersive experience, allowing you to connect with nature while still enjoying modern comforts. These camps typically feature spacious and well-appointed tents with comfortable beds, private bathrooms, and sometimes even a private deck. Some tented camps offer en-suite outdoor showers for a truly immersive bush experience. The camps often have a central dining area, lounge, and campfire, creating a communal atmosphere where guests can share stories and experiences. Tented camps provide an authentic safari experience, combining adventure with comfort.

iii. **Mid-Range Lodges and Camps:** For those seeking a balance between comfort and affordability, mid-range lodges and camps in the Masai Mara offer a great option. These accommodations provide comfortable rooms or tents with en-suite facilities, often featuring a restaurant, bar, and common areas for relaxation. While they may not offer the same level of luxury as high-end lodges, they still provide a comfortable and enjoyable stay in the Masai Mara, allowing you to experience the beauty of the reserve without breaking the bank.

iv. **Budget Campsites:** For budget-conscious travelers and those seeking a more adventurous experience, campsites are available within or near the Masai Mara. These campsites provide basic facilities such as shared bathrooms, communal cooking areas, and camping pitches. Some campsites may offer the option of renting pre-erected tents or camping gear. Camping in the Masai Mara allows you to be closer to nature, waking up to the sounds of the wilderness and gazing at the starry night sky.

v. **Exclusive-Use Private Villas:** For those looking for privacy and exclusivity, some lodges and camps in the Masai Mara offer exclusive-use private villas. These villas provide a luxurious and secluded retreat, often with private staff, a dedicated safari vehicle, and personalized services. They are ideal for families, small groups, or couples seeking a more intimate and customized experience in the Masai Mara.

When choosing where to stay in the Masai Mara, consider factors such as your budget, preferred level of comfort, location within the reserve, and the overall experience you desire. Booking accommodations in advance is recommended, especially during the peak season, to secure your preferred option and ensure a seamless safari experience.

By selecting the right accommodation that aligns with your preferences and needs, you can enhance your Masai Mara adventure and create lifelong memories in this iconic safari destination.

Masai Mara Nightlife and Entertainment

The Masai Mara is primarily known for its exceptional wildlife and breathtaking landscapes, offering visitors an immersive experience in nature. While it is not a destination renowned for its bustling nightlife and vibrant entertainment scene, there are still opportunities for evening activities and cultural experiences that can enhance your overall Masai Mara adventure. Here are some options for nightlife and entertainment in the Masai Mara:

i. **Evening Wildlife Drives:** Many safari lodges and camps in the Masai Mara offer evening game drives, allowing you to witness the nocturnal activities of the wildlife. Accompanied by experienced guides, these drives provide a unique opportunity to spot elusive creatures such as leopards, hyenas, and other nocturnal animals. The thrilling experience of venturing into the reserve after dark offers a different perspective and a chance to observe the captivating behavior of wildlife under the moonlit sky.

ii. **Cultural Performances:** To immerse yourself in the local Maasai culture, some lodges and camps organize traditional dance performances and cultural presentations in the evenings. These events often showcase Maasai songs, dances, and rituals, offering insights into their rich traditions and way of life. Engaging with the Maasai community and witnessing their vibrant performances provides a unique and authentic cultural experience.

iii. **Campfire Conversations and Stargazing:** Gather around a campfire in the evening and engage in conversations with fellow travelers, guides, or lodge staff. This is a perfect opportunity to share stories, experiences, and insights about the Masai Mara. Guides often provide interesting information about the wildlife, conservation efforts, and local culture. Additionally, the Masai Mara's remote location and limited light pollution make it an excellent place for stargazing. Marvel at the expansive night sky and be captivated by the brilliance of the stars while listening to tales of the constellations.

iv. **Relaxation and Reflection:** After a day of exciting wildlife encounters and outdoor activities, evenings in the Masai Mara offer a chance to unwind, relax, and reflect on the day's experiences. Many accommodations provide comfortable lounges, bars, or outdoor seating areas where you can enjoy a refreshing drink, savor delicious meals, or simply take in the peaceful surroundings. Use this time to connect with fellow travelers, share safari stories, or enjoy some quiet solitude amidst the natural beauty of the Masai Mara.

v. **Nighttime Nature Sounds:** As the night falls, the sounds of nature come alive in the Masai Mara.

From the distant roars of lions to the chirping of nocturnal birds and the rustling of wildlife in the bushes, the symphony of sounds creates a unique ambiance. Spend time on your lodge or camp's veranda, balcony, or outdoor seating area, and let the enchanting sounds of the African wilderness envelop you.

While the Masai Mara may not offer a bustling nightlife or extensive entertainment options, the evenings in this pristine wilderness present opportunities for cultural immersion, wildlife encounters, and relaxation. Embrace the tranquility and embrace the unique experiences that the Masai Mara provides after the sun sets, allowing you to forge a deeper connection with nature and the local culture.

Masai Mara packing list

Packing appropriately for your Masai Mara adventure is essential to ensure a comfortable and enjoyable experience in the African wilderness. From the right clothing for varying weather conditions to essential equipment for wildlife encounters, having a well-prepared packing list will help you make the most of your trip. In this guide, we will provide an introduction and details on the essential items to include in your Masai Mara packing list, ensuring you have everything you need for a successful safari adventure.

Clothing

Clothing is a crucial aspect to consider when packing for your Masai Mara trip. The right clothing will ensure comfort, protection from the elements, and appropriate attire for various activities. Here are some clothing items to include in your Masai Mara packing list:

i. **Lightweight and Breathable Shirts:** Pack lightweight, breathable shirts made of moisture-wicking fabric. Opt for long-sleeved shirts to protect yourself from the sun and insects. Light colors can help keep you cool by reflecting the sunlight.

ii. **Long Pants:** Include lightweight and comfortable long pants to protect your legs from the sun, insects, and vegetation. Convertible pants with zip-off legs are a versatile option, allowing you to adjust to different weather conditions.

iii. **Shorts or Skirts:** Pack a couple of pairs of shorts or skirts for hot days or when you're back at the lodge/camp. Make sure they are comfortable and appropriate for the cultural norms of the destination.

iv. **Sweater or Light Jacket:** Nights and early mornings in the Masai Mara can be chilly, so pack a lightweight sweater or jacket to layer over your shirts. Opt for something that can be easily packed and doesn't take up much space.

v.   **Hat and Sunglasses:** Protect your face and eyes from the sun by bringing a wide-brimmed hat and sunglasses. The hat should provide shade for your face, ears, and neck.

vi. **Comfortable Walking Shoes or Hiking Boots:** Choose sturdy, comfortable shoes or hiking boots for walking safaris and outdoor activities. Ensure they are broken-in before your trip to avoid discomfort or blisters.

vii. **Socks:** Bring a few pairs of comfortable socks suitable for walking or hiking. Consider moisture-wicking or quick-drying options to keep your feet dry and comfortable.

viii. **Swimwear:** If your accommodation has a swimming pool or offers opportunities for swimming, don't forget to pack your swimsuit.

ix. **Rain Jacket or Poncho:** Even if you visit during the dry season, it's wise to pack a lightweight rain jacket or poncho in case of unexpected showers or during the rainy season.

x. **Sleepwear:** Pack lightweight sleepwear suitable for the climate. Depending on the time of year, a light sleep sack or sleeping bag liner may be useful.

Remember to check the weather conditions and climate during your travel dates to ensure you pack the appropriate clothing. It's advisable to dress in layers, as temperatures can vary throughout the day. Additionally, consider the cultural norms and respect local customs by avoiding clothing that may be deemed inappropriate or offensive.

By packing the right clothing, you can stay comfortable, protected, and prepared for the various activities and weather conditions you'll encounter during your Masai Mara adventure.

Essential Gear and Equipment

When preparing for your Masai Mara trip, it's important to have the right gear and equipment to enhance your safari experience and ensure your comfort and safety. Here are some essential items to include in your packing list:

i. **Binoculars:** A good pair of binoculars will enhance your wildlife viewing experience by allowing you to observe animals up close, even from a distance. Look for binoculars with a magnification of at least 8x or 10x.

ii. **Camera and Extra Batteries:** Capture the incredible moments and wildlife encounters in the

Masai Mara with a reliable camera. Pack extra batteries or a portable charger to ensure you don't miss out on any photo opportunities.

iii. **Universal Power Adapter:** Carry a universal power adapter to charge your electronic devices, as the plug types and voltages may be different from what you're used to. This will ensure your devices stay powered throughout your trip.

iv. **Daypack or Backpack:** A small daypack or backpack is essential for carrying your essentials during game drives, nature walks, or excursions. It should be comfortable to wear and have enough space for your camera, binoculars, water bottle, snacks, sunscreen, and other personal items.

v. **Personal Toiletries:** Pack personal toiletries such as toothbrush, toothpaste, shampoo, conditioner, soap, and any other items you may need for your daily hygiene routine. Consider using biodegradable and environmentally-friendly products to minimize your impact on the environment.

vi. **Travel-sized First Aid Kit:** Carry a basic first aid kit that includes items such as adhesive bandages, antiseptic wipes, pain relievers, insect repellent, anti-diarrheal medication, and any necessary prescription medications. It's always better to be prepared for minor injuries or illnesses.

vii. **Flashlight or Headlamp:** A flashlight or headlamp is essential for navigating in low-light conditions, especially if you're going on evening game drives or walking safaris. Make sure to pack extra batteries or ensure it's fully charged.

viii. **Travel Wallet or Money Belt:** Keep your important documents, such as passport, travel insurance, and cash, organized and secure in a travel wallet or money belt. This will help protect your valuables and keep everything easily accessible.

ix.   **Reusable Water Bottle:** Staying hydrated is crucial during your Masai Mara adventure. Carry a reusable water bottle to minimize plastic waste and ensure you have access to clean drinking water. Some lodges and camps provide safe drinking water for refills.

x.   **Guidebooks and Maps:** Bring guidebooks and maps to familiarize yourself with the Masai Mara's wildlife, history, culture, and attractions. They can be useful references and help you make the most of your safari experience.

xi.   **Travel Locks:** Keep your luggage secure by using travel locks. This will provide an extra layer of protection for your belongings during transit and at accommodations.

xii.   **Photocopies of Important Documents:** Make photocopies or take photos of your passport, travel insurance, visa, and other important documents. Store them separately from the originals, so you have a backup in case of loss or theft.

Remember to pack efficiently and prioritize the items that are most essential for your specific needs and activities. By having the right gear and equipment, you'll be well-prepared to make the most of your Masai Mara safari adventure.

Other Important Items

In addition to clothing and essential gear, there are other important items to consider when packing for your Masai Mara trip. These items can contribute to your overall comfort, convenience, and safety during your safari adventure. Here are some additional important items to include in your packing list:

i. **Valid Passport and Travel Documents:** Ensure you have a valid passport with at least six months of validity remaining. Check visa requirements for Kenya and any other countries you may be visiting during your trip. Carry copies of your passport, travel insurance, and other important documents in case of loss or theft.

ii. **Travel Insurance:** It's highly recommended to have comprehensive travel insurance that covers medical emergencies, trip cancellation or interruption, lost or stolen belongings, and emergency medical evacuation. Review the policy coverage and contact details before your trip.

iii. **Cash and/or Credit Cards:** Carry enough cash in the local currency (Kenyan shilling) for small expenses, tips, and emergencies. It's also advisable to have a credit card or debit card for larger purchases or as a backup. Check with your bank regarding international usage and inform them of your travel plans to avoid any issues.

iv. **Guidebooks and Maps:** Bring guidebooks, maps, or travel apps that provide information about the Masai Mara, including wildlife, flora, fauna, cultural insights, and tips for getting around. These resources will enhance your understanding and appreciation of the destination.

v. **Insect Repellent:** Protect yourself from mosquitoes and other insects by packing insect repellent containing DEET or other recommended ingredients. Apply it on exposed skin to reduce the risk of mosquito-borne diseases.

vi. **Sunscreen and Sun Protection:** Carry a broad-spectrum sunscreen with a high SPF (30 or above) to protect your skin from the strong African sun. Apply it generously and frequently, especially on exposed areas. Pack a lip balm with SPF as well.

Additionally, bring a lightweight, wide-brimmed hat, sunglasses, and lightweight clothing that provide UPF (Ultraviolet Protection Factor).

vii. **Medications and Personal Health Supplies:** If you take prescription medications, ensure you have an adequate supply for the duration of your trip. Pack any necessary over-the-counter medications for common ailments such as headaches, allergies, motion sickness, and digestive issues. Consider packing a basic first aid kit with band-aids, antiseptic ointment, and other essentials.

viii. **Snacks and Water Purification:** Carry some energy bars, trail mix, or other non-perishable snacks to keep you fueled during long game drives or when hiking. Additionally, if you plan to drink water from natural sources, bring water purification tablets or a portable water filter to ensure it's safe for consumption.

ix.   **Travel Towel:** Pack a lightweight, quick-drying travel towel that takes up less space than regular towels. It will come in handy for drying off after activities, as well as for picnics or as a makeshift blanket.

x.   **Mobile Phone and Chargers:** Bring your mobile phone and charger to stay connected and capture photos and videos. Ensure your phone is unlocked or check with your service provider for international roaming options. Portable chargers or power banks can be useful when you're on the go and don't have access to electrical outlets.

xi.   **Travel Adapters:** Check the type of electrical outlets in Kenya and bring the necessary travel adapters to charge your electronic devices. Adapters may vary depending on your home country.

xii.   **Reusable Bags:** Carry reusable bags or lightweight foldable daypacks for shopping, storing dirty or wet clothes, or collecting any trash during your excursions. This will help reduce plastic waste and keep your belongings organized.

xiii. **Entertainment and Travel Comfort:** Pack items such as books, magazines, or travel games to keep yourself entertained during downtime or when traveling. Consider bringing a travel pillow, earplugs, and an eye mask for added comfort during flights or long drives.

xiv.   **Extra Set of Clothes:** It's always a good idea to have an extra set of clothes in your carry-on or daypack in case of delays, lost luggage, or unexpected situations.

Remember to check the specific requirements and recommendations of your tour operator or accommodations, as well as any additional items you may need based on the activities and duration of your stay in the Masai Mara. By packing these important items, you'll be prepared for a comfortable, convenient, and enjoyable safari adventure.

Don't forget to pack light and prioritize essentials. Check the weather forecast before your trip and adjust your packing list accordingly. Also, consider any specific requirements or recommendations from your tour operator or accommodation. By being well-prepared with the right gear and essentials, you can make the most of your Masai Mara adventure and enjoy a comfortable and hassle-free safari experience.

Top attractive place in Masai Mara

The Masai Mara is a captivating destination in Africa that offers a wealth of natural beauty and remarkable wildlife encounters. Known for its vast savannahs, diverse ecosystems, and abundant wildlife, the Masai Mara is home to several attractive places that draw visitors from around the world. From the iconic Maasai Mara National Reserve to the picturesque Mara River and beyond, there are numerous must-visit locations that showcase the splendor of this incredible destination. In this guide, we will introduce you to some of the top attractive places in the Masai Mara, each offering its own unique allure and memorable experiences.

i. **Maasai Mara National Reserve:** The Maasai Mara National Reserve is the centerpiece of the Masai Mara region and one of the most famous wildlife destinations in Africa. Spanning over 1,500 square kilometers, it is renowned for its abundant wildlife, including the Big Five (lion, leopard, elephant, buffalo, and rhinoceros), wildebeest migration, and diverse bird species. The reserve offers stunning vistas of rolling grasslands, riverine forests, and dramatic savannahs, providing exceptional game viewing opportunities.

ii. **Mara River:** The Mara River is an iconic feature of the Masai Mara, known for its dramatic wildebeest river crossings during the Great Migration. Witnessing thousands of wildebeest and zebra braving the crocodile-infested waters is a truly unforgettable experience. The river is also home to hippopotamuses and numerous bird species, making it a captivating destination for wildlife enthusiasts and photographers.

iii. **Talek River:** The Talek River is another significant river in the Masai Mara, and it serves as a vital water source for the wildlife in the area. It offers opportunities to spot various animal species, including crocodiles, hippos, and a wide array of birdlife. The scenic beauty of the Talek River, with its meandering course and lush vegetation, adds to the charm of the Masai Mara.

iv. **Olare Orok Conservancy:** Located adjacent to the Maasai Mara National Reserve, the Olare Orok Conservancy is a private conservancy that offers a more exclusive and intimate safari experience. It is known for its low tourist density, pristine wilderness, and a wide variety of wildlife. The conservancy provides an opportunity for night game drives and walking safaris, offering a unique perspective on the Masai Mara ecosystem.

v. **Mara Triangle:** The Mara Triangle is a western sector of the Maasai Mara National Reserve. It is known for its breathtaking landscapes, including the Siria Escarpment, Oloololo Ridge, and Mara River. The area boasts excellent wildlife sightings, particularly during the Great Migration. Visitors can enjoy game drives, guided walks, and picnics while taking in the stunning views of the Mara Triangle.

vi. **Musiara Swamp:** The Musiara Swamp is a lush wetland area in the Masai Mara that attracts a variety of wildlife, especially during the dry season. It is a favorite grazing spot for herbivores such as elephants, buffalos, and giraffes, which, in turn, attract predators like lions and hyenas. The swamp is also a paradise for birdwatchers, with a myriad of bird species calling it home.

vii. **Ol Kinyei Conservancy:** The Ol Kinyei Conservancy is a community-based wildlife conservancy that offers a unique blend of wildlife conservation and cultural experiences. It is known for its diverse wildlife population, including elephants, cheetahs, leopards, and abundant birdlife. Visitors can participate in game drives, guided walks, and cultural visits to local Maasai villages.

viii. **Mara Naboisho Conservancy:** The Mara Naboisho Conservancy is a private conservancy that promotes sustainable tourism and wildlife conservation. It offers a tranquil and exclusive safari experience with excellent game viewing opportunities. Visitors can enjoy guided nature walks, night game drives, and bush picnics while supporting community initiatives.

These are just a few of the many attractive places in the Masai Mara. Each location offers unique experiences and opportunities to witness the incredible wildlife and stunning landscapes that make the Masai Mara a world-class safari destination. Exploring these captivating attractions will leave you with unforgettable memories of your time in this remarkable corner of Africa.

Masia Mara post Covid-19

The COVID-19 pandemic has had a significant impact on travel and tourism worldwide, including the Masai Mara. As destinations around the world gradually reopen and adapt to the new normal, the Masai Mara has implemented measures to prioritize the safety and well-being of visitors while ensuring a memorable and enjoyable safari experience. Here is an overview of what you can expect when visiting the Masai Mara post COVID-19:

i. **Health and Safety Protocols:** The Masai Mara has implemented enhanced health and safety protocols in line with guidelines from health authorities and government regulations. These measures may include temperature screenings, hand sanitization stations, social distancing guidelines, and increased sanitation practices in accommodations, vehicles, and public areas.

ii. **Limited Tourist Numbers:** To maintain physical distancing and minimize crowding, there may be restrictions on the number of visitors allowed in certain areas of the Masai Mara, including game drives and attractions. It is advisable to check with your tour operator or accommodation in advance and make reservations accordingly.

iii. **Accommodation Safety Measures:** Lodges, camps, and other accommodations have implemented enhanced cleaning and sanitization protocols to ensure the safety of guests. Common areas, dining facilities, and guest rooms are regularly cleaned and sanitized, with particular attention to high-touch surfaces.

iv. **Flexible Booking and Cancellation Policies:** Many accommodations and tour operators have revised their booking and cancellation policies to provide more flexibility in light of uncertain travel conditions. This allows travelers to make changes or cancellations if necessary due to COVID-19-related circumstances.

v. **Local Community Engagement:** The Masai Mara has always valued the participation and support of local communities. Post-COVID-19, there may be increased efforts to engage and involve local communities in tourism activities, ensuring that the benefits of tourism are shared and sustainable.

vi. **Wildlife Conservation:** The pandemic has highlighted the importance of wildlife conservation and the need to protect natural habitats. The Masai Mara continues its commitment to wildlife conservation efforts, and visitors may have the opportunity to learn more about these initiatives and contribute to conservation projects.

vii. **Responsible Travel Practices:** Travelers are encouraged to practice responsible tourism by respecting wildlife, following park rules and regulations, supporting local communities, and minimizing their impact on the environment. This includes avoiding littering, staying on designated trails, and adhering to wildlife viewing guidelines.

It's important to stay informed about travel restrictions, entry requirements, and health guidelines issued by local authorities and governments before planning your visit to the Masai Mara. Check with your travel agent, tour operator, or the official websites of relevant authorities for the latest information.

While the post-COVID-19 travel experience may involve additional precautions and changes, the Masai Mara's natural beauty, wildlife, and cultural experiences remain as enchanting as ever. By adhering to safety guidelines and practicing responsible travel, you can enjoy a memorable and safe safari adventure in the Masai Mara.

Top Masia Mara meals you have to try out

When visiting the Masai Mara, you'll have the opportunity to savor a variety of delicious meals that showcase the flavors of Kenya and the region. From traditional dishes to contemporary culinary creations, here are some top Masai Mara meals you have to try out:

i. **Nyama Choma:** Nyama Choma is a popular Kenyan dish that consists of grilled or roasted meat, typically goat or beef. The meat is marinated with spices and cooked over an open fire, resulting in flavorful and tender bites. It is often served with a side of Ugali (a cornmeal-based staple) and accompanied by a variety of sauces and condiments.

ii. **Ugali and Sukuma Wiki:** Ugali is a staple food in Kenya, made from maize flour and cooked into a thick, dough-like consistency. It is often served with Sukuma Wiki, a delicious vegetable dish made from collard greens or kale, cooked with onions, tomatoes, and spices. The combination of Ugali and Sukuma Wiki is a satisfying and traditional Kenyan meal.

iii. **Chapati and Curry:** Chapati is a type of flatbread that is widely enjoyed in Kenya. It is made from wheat flour, oil, and water, and is cooked on a griddle. Chapati is often paired with flavorful curries, such as chicken, beef, or vegetable curry, which are rich in spices and aromatic flavors. This combination makes for a tasty and filling meal.

iv. **Pilau:** Pilau is a fragrant and spiced rice dish that is commonly prepared in Kenya. It is made with basmati rice cooked with a blend of spices, including cumin, cardamom, cinnamon, and cloves. Pilau often incorporates meat or vegetables, creating a flavorful one-pot meal that is enjoyed by locals and visitors alike.

v.   **Mandazi:** Mandazi is a popular Kenyan snack or breakfast item. It is a type of deep-fried bread that is slightly sweet and often flavored with coconut milk or cardamom. Mandazi is typically enjoyed with a cup of tea or coffee and can be found in local markets, roadside stalls, and even at some lodges and camps in the Masai Mara.

vi.   **Fresh Tropical Fruits:** Kenya is blessed with an abundance of fresh tropical fruits, and the Masai Mara region is no exception. Indulge in the flavors of juicy mangoes, pineapples, passion fruits, papayas, and more. These fruits make for refreshing snacks or desserts that will tantalize your taste buds.

vii.   **Kenyan Tea and Coffee:** Kenya is renowned for its tea and coffee production. Enjoy a cup of Kenyan tea, which is often served hot with milk and sugar. You can also savor the richness and aroma of Kenyan coffee, which is grown in the highlands of the country. These beverages are a delightful way to start your day or take a break during your Masai Mara adventure.

When dining in the Masai Mara, you'll find a range of options that cater to different tastes and dietary preferences. Many lodges and camps offer diverse menus that include international cuisines alongside local Kenyan dishes. Whether you're enjoying a meal at your accommodation, joining a bush dinner under the stars, or visiting local restaurants, be sure to explore the flavors of the Masai Mara and indulge in these delectable meals that showcase the vibrant culinary heritage of Kenya.

Conclusion

In conclusion, the Masai Mara is a mesmerizing destination that offers a truly unforgettable safari experience. With its extraordinary wildlife, stunning landscapes, and rich cultural heritage, it has rightfully earned its place as one of Africa's premier safari destinations. From witnessing the Great Migration to immersing yourself in the vibrant Maasai culture, there is so much to explore and discover in this remarkable corner of Kenya.

When planning your trip to the Masai Mara, it's important to consider the best time to visit, taking into account the wildlife migrations and weather patterns. Each month offers unique experiences and highlights, allowing you to tailor your visit to your preferences and interests.

While in the Masai Mara, make the most of your time by engaging in activities that showcase the region's extraordinary wildlife. Whether it's embarking on game drives to spot the Big Five, witnessing the Great

Migration, or immersing yourself in birdwatching and photography opportunities, the wildlife encounters are sure to leave you in awe. Beyond wildlife experiences, the Masai Mara offers cultural immersion opportunities where you can engage with the local Maasai communities, learn about their traditions, and support their sustainable initiatives. These interactions provide a deeper understanding of the region's cultural heritage and enrich your overall travel experience. Ensuring your safety and well-being in the Masai Mara is paramount. Adhering to park rules and regulations, respecting wildlife, and practicing responsible travel are essential to preserving the delicate ecosystems and ensuring a sustainable future for the Masai Mara.

When it comes to planning your trip, familiarize yourself with the visa requirements and necessary travel documents. Consider consulting with the Kenyan Embassy or Consulate for up-to-date information and guidance. Additionally, having a well-prepared packing list, including appropriate clothing, essential gear, and personal items, will ensure your comfort and convenience throughout your journey. Choosing suitable accommodation in the Masai Mara is crucial for a memorable stay. From luxury lodges to eco-friendly camps, there are various options that cater to different preferences and budgets. Selecting accommodations that prioritize sustainability and offer unique experiences will enhance your connection with nature and the local environment.

Ultimately, a trip to the Masai Mara is an opportunity to immerse yourself in the wonders of nature, witness extraordinary wildlife, and create lifelong memories. It's a chance to appreciate the delicate balance between humans and wildlife, and to contribute to conservation efforts and the well-being of local communities. By embracing the breathtaking landscapes, incredible wildlife, and vibrant culture of the Masai Mara, you will embark on an adventure that will leave a lasting impact and foster a deep appreciation for the beauty and diversity of our natural world. So, plan your journey, embrace the magic of the Masai Mara, and prepare for an unforgettable safari experience like no other.

Printed in Great Britain
by Amazon

39223922R00155